AIDS AND THE SLEEPING CHURCH

7-9-18

In the late 1970s Dr. John Frame MD
of the NCCCUSA already alerted
the church to prepare for
the epidemics of AIDS.

"Stay awake and pray …"   Matthew 26:41

AIDS
and the
SLEEPING CHURCH

Patricia L. Hoffman

Foreword by
Chris Glaser

William B. Eerdmans Publishing Company

Grand Rapids, Michigan
Cambridge, England

Cover art by John August Swanson
Agony in the Garden 1989
Watercolor 20 x 14 inches
Courtesy of Bergsma Gallery, Grand Rapids, MI

Poems and prayers used with permission of the authors.

William B. Eerdmans Publishing Company
255 Jefferson Ave. SE   P.O. Box 163
Grand Rapids, MI 49503   Cambridge CB3 9PU U.K.
All rights reserved

Printed in the United States of America

Library of Congress Cataloging-in-Publication Data
Hoffman, Particia L., (Patricia Louise). 1935–
AIDS and the Sleeping Church / Patricia L. Hoffman : foreword by Chris Glaser.
p. cm.
ISBN 0–8028–4069–8 (alk. paper)
1. Church work with the sick. 2. Hoffman, Patricia L. (Patricia Louise). 1935
— Diaries. 3. Presbyterians — United States — Diaries. 4. AIDS (Disease) —
Patients — Religious life. 5. AIDS (Disease) — Patients — Pastoral counseling
of. 6. AIDS (Disease) — Religious aspects — Christianity.   I. Title.
BV4460.7.H63   1995   95–36887
261.8'321969792–dc20   CIP

To Cecil, my companion on life's journey

Contents

Foreword

"Keep awake, therefore, for you do not know on what day your Lord is coming." Matthew 24:42
Thus Jesus warned the disciples, lest they be caught unawares by his return.
"Stay awake and pray ..." Matthew 26:41
Thus Jesus enjoined His disciples while he suffered agony in the garden of Gethsemane.

For the most part, the church has been caught sleeping while Christ has returned in the guise of persons with AIDS. The church has resisted praying with them in their personal Gethsemanes, to visit them during their illness.

Mother Teresa has recognized a leper as "Christ in a distressing disguise." And, overcoming a phobia about leprosy, Francis of Assisi hugged a leper and later realized it was Christ himself.

People with AIDS are treated as the lepers of our time: unvisited, unrecognized, and unhugged by many Christians.

Yet Pat Hoffman's Christian faith brought her to visit persons with AIDS, recognizing their sacred worth and offering them much-needed hugs. In return, she received their ministry: one that taught her about her own life, reminded her of her own sacred worth, and embraced her with God's unconditional love. In no church could she have better heard the words of assurance that one of her new friends with AIDS proclaimed, "Just be you."

However else my good friend Pat may pray, I know that her primary prayer with people with AIDS is simple presence. Pat is a disciple alert to human need, refusing to abandon those agonizing in their own Gethsemanes. In being so, she has discerned God's will for her own life. Day by day, her journal's simple style reveals profound spiritual insight for our lives, too. Her's is a spirituality that goes beyond mere religion.

Throughout her life, Pat Hoffman has tried to awaken the sleeping church to all kinds of human need. With this journal she hopes to alert Christians like herself to the need of serving individuals and families with AIDS, and the ensuing personal fulfillment.

When AIDS surfaced in the early 1980s, I urged members of a clergy group to become involved in ministry with persons with AIDS. The ministers were hesitant, maybe afraid of the disease itself, but also concerned over what other Christians might think if they were to get involved. They knew that the segments of the population most affected by AIDS were those to whom the church had offered condemnation rather than kindness. Some preachers had even declared AIDS as God's punishment for homosexuality. Would those judged so unmercifully welcome the church's ministry?

One pastor who did respond volunteered to be an "AIDS buddy" through a social service agency. The program was established to meet the physical needs of clients with AIDS, such as housecleaning, shopping, transportation to medical appointments — whatever was needed. When the pastor met his first "buddy" by phone, he tried to avoid revealing his vocation. Finally the young man asked, "What sort of work do you do?" When my friend replied that he was a minister the young man shot back, "I hope you're not going to dump any religious garbage on me!" The minister quickly assured him that that was not his mission.

Yet, during the minister's initial visit, the first question the young man asked was, "Do you suppose this is some kind of punishment from God?" So, even though he hadn't wanted any religious "garbage" dumped on him, he was dealing with such tough spiritual questions.

I once spoke on the spiritual dimensions of the AIDS crisis with social workers assigned to marginalized and often homeless people with AIDS. One therapist described a client who refused medical help, resisted taking medication, and was suicidal. "I tried every trick in the psychotherapeutic book to get him to turn around, to choose life, but nothing worked," she said. Finally, the therapist, who described herself as "nominally Jewish" and somewhat suspicious of religion, decided to — in her own words — "use the F word: Faith." She encouraged him to talk about his boyhood Christian faith, and wound up tapping spiritual resources to help him face the challenge of AIDS.

To use John the Baptist's metaphor, people living with AIDS are sifting the grain from the dross of their faith, discerning what is vital for Christian living and what is unnecessary, even harmful. Just as Jesus sifted through his own tradition to explain the heart of being faithful, so those facing their own Gethsemanes search for God's will as they suffer. We are called, like Jesus' disciples, to be there for them and to pray with them.

We cannot anticipate the results of either our presence or our prayer. Neither can be used to mold people the way we want. A person with AIDS who formerly belonged to a campus Christian group once told me that the worst insult its members could hurl at one another was, *"I will pray for you."* That meant the speaker intended to conform your belief or behavior to their's through prayer.

Our ministry may not bring the healing we expect. During an interfaith conference on AIDS in Fort Worth, Texas, a Nazarene stood to say that he never experienced healing until his diagnosis of AIDS. When he risked telling his family, his home church, and his hometown that he was a gay man with AIDS, he found all welcomed him home. He described this as the most healing moment of his life.

Our ministry may not heal others of their illness, but it may transform us as healers. When my father died of cancer, my mother doubted the efficacy of her prayers. Yet I believe that praying for my father made her a better caregiver.

In Gethsemane, an anguished Jesus begged God for the cup to pass from him. His disciples thought that "to be there" for him was to deny his perilous destiny, or to swear they'd never betray or deny him, or to take out a sword and attack one of those who came to take him. Yet what Jesus requested of them was only to share a meal with him, sing a hymn with him, pray with him.

In entering the Gethsemanes of those hospitalized with AIDS, Pat Hoffman found herself required to do little more than be there, alert and awake to subtle and not-so-subtle expressions of joy, hope, fear, pain, pleasure, and love. Through Pat's journal, readers are invited to enter the gardens not only of persons struggling with AIDS, but her own garden of suffering and joy. There we may discern the Christ and hear the gospel proclaimed by people living with AIDS: Live with grace, live with humor, live with integrity, live with love, live with hope, live with yourself.

Chris Glaser
Atlanta, Georgia

Chris Glaser, M.Div., is the author of four books —
most recently, *The Word is Out* and *Coming Out to God*.

Acknowledgments

I wish to thank all my friends and loved ones who read the journal while it was in progress and gave valuable critiques, especially Greg Dobie who read every word and gave significant input and encouragement. I'm indebted to readers of the manuscript who care about persons with AIDS and who let me know how the journal touched them.

I want to give special thanks to artist John Swanson, who carries his friends in his heart and makes things happen. I am grateful to Chris Glaser, who in the unfolding of our friendship over many years has influenced the direction of my life and work.

I want to acknowledge the importance to me of the support of those who loved the people in this journal, especially Bob and Alice. I hope the journal honors the final months of life and struggle for the people dear to them.

I am grateful to Ivy Dempsey, Matthew Garrison, Carol Hamilton, and Perry Wiggins who contributed poetry and prayers for the book.

My special thanks to Sandra DeGroot, Eerdmans' Project Developer, who so deeply understands my writing, whose vision helped shape this book, whose commitment to love and inclusivity powered the development of the book, and whose comprehensive skills brought together a wonderful editor, Andy Angelo, John Swanson's cover art, and Aaron Phipps' page designs.

My final thanks are to all those spoken of in the journal who invited me into their lives. May the journal entries be votive candles lit in your remembrance.

Introduction

Recently, I conducted a memorial service for a man who had died of AIDS. Six years ago I could not have imagined myself in that role. I'm a Presbyterian laywoman who has been more involved with social justice than liturgy. I was more knowledgeable about the farm labor movement than about coping with grief. But my life was profoundly affected by the people you will meet in my journal, people with AIDS, their mothers, fathers, friends and mates.

I kept this journal in 1989 during the first months I was visiting AIDS patients at Daniel Freeman Marina Hospital at Marina del Rey in Los Angeles.

I took on this work because I was needing to find a new direction in my career and thought some volunteer work would give me a taste of something different. For many years I had been involved in ecumenical social justice work. I was an activist and writer on justice issues.

But at 53 I was coming to terms with the limits of activism in my body and spirit. I had been laid up for months following each of two knee surgeries and then a hysterectomy. I had become aware of my feelings of helplessness when I couldn't be as active as I was used to. I needed to pay attention to those helpless feelings and how I had defended against them.

I was living in Los Angeles, which had been hard hit by the acquired immunodeficiency syndrome, the AIDS epidemic. I have gay and lesbian friends in the church and their suffering with losses to AIDS brought the reality close to me. I wanted to be involved. Since the church was on the sidelines of the epidemic, my involvement was as an AIDS Project Los Angeles (APLA) hospital volunteer.

I invite you into that involvement by accompanying me down the halls of Daniel Freeman Marina Hospital to meet people affected by AIDS. You probably already are acquainted with people affected by AIDS, in your church, your neighborhood, at work, but you may not know it. Because of the continuing stigma, people often keep quiet.

I've stayed in touch with some of the parents of people mentioned in the journal. One couple, a clergyman and his wife, said they never told their congregation the cause of their son's death. They feared the reaction. The woman said it would have helped them if they could have talked openly about their grief and been comforted by their Christian community.

My own journey after leaving the volunteer work at Daniel Freeman Marina Hospital took me to a position at the AIDS Research and Education Project at California State University, Long Beach, where I helped develop and implement a physician education program for their care of patients with HIV infection. After my husband, Cecil, and I moved out of Los Angeles to Ventura, Calif., I was accepted into a Clinical Pastoral Education program where I received training in chaplaincy. For more than two years I have been a chaplain to persons with HIV disease in Ventura County.

How did this Presbyterian laywoman in her 50s move from being a hospital volunteer to being a chaplain? I invite you now into my journal to meet some of the people who altered the course of my life.

Journal

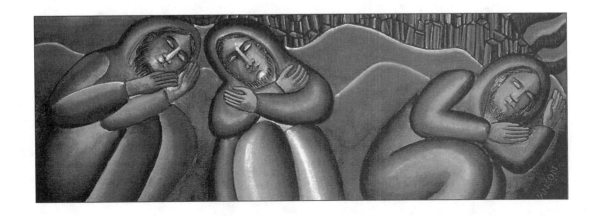

Thursday, May 18, 1989

I began today. I felt uncomfortable and a bit lost starting at the hospital. In the APLA volunteer training we were told to always check in with the charge nurse when arriving on the unit, but I don't even know who that is. I'll have to find out these things and hope I don't insult too many people in my ignorance.

When I arrived at Daniel Freeman Marina Hospital, I drove into the back parking lot, which is reserved for staff and volunteers. I entered through the back door, trying to recall from the tour I had taken just how to get to the volunteers' office. I found it, right next to the lobby. I signed my name in the book and was given a temporary badge. A permanent one will come later.

I walked down the hall past one restricted hallway going off to the left and found the oncology unit where AIDS patients (or HIV patients as they are called at the hospital) are treated. It's called Unit 500. I reported to Pat, the unit secretary, and told her I was there to do my volunteer work. She phoned Byrle, the unit supervisor, then told me to wait. I wandered down the hall and noted how many HIV patients were on the floor and identified the room of one man I had heard about from another volunteer and whom I had promised to see.

Byrle came hurrying along to the nurses' station. He is a big teddy bear of a man. He welcomed me, and while we stood at the nurses' station he began introducing me to everyone who came by. I had no idea how any of them fit into the picture, if they were all attached somehow to Unit 500 or worked in other parts of the hospital.

I began to feel at home when Byrle took me down the hall and introduced me to some patients. The first patient, David, must be in his late 20s. Byrle introduced me as the new volunteer from APLA. David's handsome, pale face warmed with a smile. He raised himself from the bed on his left arm and stuck his hand out to shake mine. I felt this was a test to see if I would touch him. I did.

In the next room Byrle introduced me to Tom, the man I had promised to see, and his lover, Robert, who was visiting. Tom is a client of APLA and wanted to get help drawing up a will. Byrle left me there to talk with them. I sat down, glad to have something useful to do. Tom said he didn't own much, but what he had he wanted to leave to Robert. His only relative, he said, was his father and they had been estranged for years.

While Tom and Robert and I talked, Tom shook uncontrollably from a fever. He was covered with blankets up to his chin. Robert kept gently caressing Tom's blanket-covered arms.

When I left, I returned to the nurses' station and sat uncomfortably wondering what else to do. Martha, one of the nurses I had met earlier, was busy filling forms out, but seeing me there she told me she would introduce me to the other patients as soon as she finished some record keeping.

After a few minutes she took me down the hall to meet Neal and his mother, who was from Bellevue, Washington. Neal looked awfully sick and didn't feel like talking. He had a nose tube to help his breathing. He resembled his mother. They both had brown hair with a lot of body. Her's was flecked with gray. Neal's was cut in a butch and it had grown out quite a bit.

His mother said she and her husband were going home that evening. I had an urge to tell Neal I could be around like a substitute mother, but I knew that really wasn't true. I was a comma inserted into this man's life. I knew nothing of what had gone before or how it affected the present. And no one knew what would follow my comma of a moment.

Martha guided me off the hall where the patient rooms are located to an adjacent patio to introduce me to Mark, his mother, Alice, and Mark's dog, Arlo. I have never been in a hospital where dogs could visit. It was obviously a comfort and joy for Mark to see Arlo. I learned that Alice is from out of town and has been staying at Mark's home, which he shares with his lover of 10 years. Back home Alice does AIDS volunteer work. Her routine while she's here in Los Angeles is to come to the hospital each morning with the newspaper and to come again in the early afternoon to bring Mark's dog for a visit on the patio.

Mark's an attractive man in his 30s, tall and slender, with sandy brown hair and eyes to match. The light brown of his eyes was just the color I remember my father's eyes to be. Mark was dressed in lightweight sweatpants and a knit shirt. He talked a lot. He has a small, interestingly mobile mouth. Words don't just fall from his lips. Rather, his mouth sends them out through the air.

We sat in the sun. He talked about his work as an architect and how he had finally left the firm he had been with to reduce the stress in his life. He talked about the help he had gotten from Shanti, an emotional support organization serving people with HIV infection. He spoke of how he had thought his lover would leave him when he was diagnosed three years before. But his lover, Bob, had stayed and supported him. He explained about his problems with his health insurer and the valuable assistance of a knowledgable insurance counselor at APLA. And he talked about the people who have died, including a man who had given him psychological counseling when he was first diagnosed. That man had been important to him.

"I was sitting in a coffee shop in Palm Springs reading the paper. And there was my counselor's name in the obituaries," Mark recalled. "I shed a few tears right there in the coffee shop. He had died of AIDS."

I had been at the hospital two hours and was walking down the hall, ready to leave. Neal's mother came walking toward me. I stopped and said, "It must be hard to leave." She acknowledged that it was, but they had to get back home. She mentioned wishing Neal's Presbyterian church was more active in visiting him. She seemed so happy to discover that my husband is a Presbyterian clergyman and had some things in common with her and her husband that she rushed me down the hall to meet Neal's father, who seemed relieved to carry on even a brief conversation about more comfortable topics related to the church.

Then he said to Neal concerning his congregation, "They ought to bring you communion." With embarrassment he quickly added, "Not last rites or anything, just communion." Turning to me he said, "Neal was ordained an elder." Neal, who was sitting up on the bed, trying to get air and get comfortable, managed to interject, "That was a long time ago."

By the end of the afternoon, I felt somewhat rooted, not in the hospital so much as with the people. In a short time I had become involved in the lives of quite a few people. I appreciated the way they had so comfortably included me, as though I really had a place in this setting.

Sunday, May 21

I wanted to go by to see Neal for a few minutes. I had been thinking about how sick he was and that he might be missing his parents. So this afternoon I went by to see him, carrying with me a red rose from our garden.

He was very ill and whispered to me that he had a fever. I touched his forehead. My hand felt cool against his hot forehead. He reached up, took my hand and held it tight against his chest. We stayed that way in silence. After a few minutes he began to cough. I got him some water. He sat up to drink it. Then I told him I was going and would see him in a couple of days. He looked at the rose and with great effort he said, "The flower is beautiful. God be with you."

Who is being ministered to here?

Monday, May 22

In the late morning, my husband, Cecil, and I took our bicycles to the marina for a pleasant spring ride, followed by a picnic at Burton Chace Park with a view of the pleasure boats lined up in their slips.

As I had been riding along on my bicycle in the sun and breeze, I had thought of Neal and the others at the hospital. A feeling of guilt swept over me.

But I remembered something I read by Matthew Fox, the Dominican who writes from a creation spirituality. All good gifts and blessings come from God. We would seem ungrateful if we didn't enjoy the gifts and give thanks.

So I gave thanks for the bicycle ride and picnic with my husband. And I gave thanks for David and Tom and Neal and Mark. They are alive and doing their work of being who they are, although they are limited to a bed, a small room, and maybe a corridor.

Tuesday, May 23

Tuesdays and Thursdays are the days I visit at the hospital. I go in the afternoons. Things are seeming more familiar. Today I looked for the nurses I had already met and asked about the HIV patients. Were there any new ones? Yes, two. One had not been diagnosed, the other was in denial, I was told. Mark had been discharged. I was happy for him and for his mother. She wasn't going back to her home until Mark was settled and feeling better.

I went first to see Neal. His fever was down to about 100 degrees. He still spoke in a whisper and with effort. We talked a little about his parents. He let me know he had a good relationship with them and they were coming back to Los Angeles to be with him on the weekend. I asked about people from his congregation, had they been visiting him? He said, some. How had that been, I asked? He hesitated and then said they were "pushy."

It was such an effort for him to talk that I didn't explore these matters further, but I wondered. What did he mean when he said visitors from his church were pushy? I could imagine some scenarios because I am familiar with that congregation. The visitors may have wanted to "save his soul" before he died. But I could only guess.

I asked if there was anything I could do for him. He wanted me to have a nurse phone a man from his church to ask him not to come. I got his small address book from the bedside table. He labored over finding the number, then said that it was probably too late, the visitor would be on his way, but he asked if the nurse would ask the man to leave after about 10 minutes. I would convey his request.

Before I left, I let him know that a pastor, sensitive on gay and lesbian issues, was nearby — and I happened to know, being part of the Presbyterian network, that he knew Neal's parents. Would Neal like the pastor to contact his parents while they were in Los Angeles for the weekend? He looked surprised that this man, whom he had known as a child, was nearby. He said, "Just five minutes away?" I said yes, just five minutes away. "I'll call him if you want me to." He nodded yes. Then he said he was ready to rest.

Throughout this conversation he was holding my hand. Or was I holding his? He was lying on top of the covers in his hospital gown. His legs were young and strong. I noticed his feet and ankles seemed swollen. I wondered why.

I went to see Tom. He had gotten news the day before that he has two serious diseases which have attacked now that his immune system is almost gone. "It's the beginning of the end," he said. He didn't seem depressed, but he seemed realistic and sad. "Mostly I fear the pain," he said. "Are you in pain now?" I asked. He said no, but it would be painful at the end. "But they will give me Demerol to keep me somewhat comfortable."

The next day Tom was expecting someone to visit him who would help him draw up a will and sign power of attorney papers. "It will set my mind at ease to have that done," he told me.

Thursday morning, 11 a.m., May 25

I got a phone call at home from the social worker at the hospital. "Pat, I wanted to let you know before you came in this afternoon that Neal has died," she told me. I hung up and immediately began to cry. I was surprised at my tears. I felt I needed to do something, needed to get closure.

Maybe I just wanted activity to blunt the sorrow. I phoned Reverend David Meekhof, the minister who was planning to visit Neal and his parents the next day, and told him the news. I suggested he call Neal's parents. Then I realized I was one of the last people to talk with Neal and decided to write the letter below to his parents and share that last conversation.

I'm the hospital volunteer you met last Thursday in Neal's room. I just received a call from the hospital letting me know Neal died on Tuesday afternoon. I had seen him on Sunday and earlier on Tuesday and wanted to share those experiences with you because they speak of what a kind, affectionate, caring young man he was.

I dropped by the hospital briefly last Sunday just to see Neal and bring him a red rose from the garden. He had a raging fever and could barely speak. He remembered me and whispered, "I have a fever." I put my hand on his brow. He took it and held it tight to his chest. I think, for those few minutes, I was a stand-in in the family of faith for you, his beloved parents. As I was getting ready to leave, he looked at the flower and commented that it was beautiful. He was so thoughtful.

Tuesday afternoon I was back for my regular volunteer hours. When I got to Neal's room he looked a little better, but still could hardly speak. He held my hand and we managed to have a short conversation.

He asked how the other guys were doing. Apparently a nurse had taken him down the hall occasionally. On the very day he died, he was asking about other patients on the unit.

He spoke of his good relationship with you both. I told him Reverend David Meekhof was located only five minutes away and I knew he used to be your pastor. Would Neal like for me to contact Rev. Meekhof so he could see you when you came down on the weekend? He nodded yes that he would like that. Then he told me he was ready to rest and I left the room.

All the nursing staff were fond of Neal and commented on how sweet he was. And he surely won my heart.

I am sorry he is gone from this world. But God's grace working through you produced a loving son. The love and care he demonstrated to the very end will continue to bless people.

My own tears accompany this letter.

Pat Hoffman

Thursday evening

I had known Neal for five days, had spent maybe altogether 45 minutes with him. How could his death so affect me? But there was, with only a few words, an intensity. He allowed me into the circle of his life in simple, direct ways during the last two days of his life. He held on to me, did not, could not, hide his suffering. I had come to share it and he allowed it.

"I have thrush," he said, and displayed the fungus on his tongue. "Does that create some swelling," I asked? "Yes," he said. "I have a fever," and I touched his head.

When I walked in the back door of the hospital this afternoon I was wondering how the nurses handle the deaths of their patients. I had never thought about it before. I wondered what ways are available to them to express their grief and to bring closure with that person and his family.

I took along a card with my letter and hesitantly asked if any of the nursing staff would like to sign the card. All through the afternoon, as nurses came and went, they were writing notes and signing the card. It became an occasion for talking about Neal and his death. He was a special patient to them, always considerate and, from all reports, fun.

I was shocked to discover that he had died just as I was leaving the hospital on Tuesday afternoon at 4 o'clock. I wished I had stayed five more minutes, but I don't know why. I don't understand my own desire to have been there at the end.

His nurse told me that he had rung for her and said he wasn't feeling well. When she checked him out he was in respiratory arrest. There was an urgent overhead page of "code blue" notifying medical personnel to come immediately to his room. The crash cart with emergency equipment came tearing down the hallway. The other patients who have been around awhile know what that means. The nurses didn't know what happened nor why he died when he did. "Afterwards, we just lost it," said his nurse. "We were crying. Our supervisor said, 'OK, this is it. Time out.'" But almost immediately, they put someone else in his room," Neal's nurse said. "I think they ought to retire a room for a day or two. I can't handle going into that room."

Friday, May 26

The first patient I had met was David. When I saw David yesterday he seemed weaker. He told me he can't get out of bed. He seemed depressed. I was uncomfortable with allowing whatever feelings were there in him to surface. This is an old family pattern — when faced with sadness and discouragement, be cheerful. So, I commented on the beautiful potted freesias on the table at the end of his bed. He said, "My sister gave them to me. I only wish I could smell them." I offered to bring them over to him; he said he would like that. Freesias grow on long stems with several little trumpet-like flowers to each stem. He had two kinds, white and orange. I brought the orange freesias to him. David gently gathered a cluster of flowers in his hands and held them close to his face. He kept smelling them with his eyes closed. Then he cupped his hands around another cluster and took in their delicate fragrance. In the midst of his pain and deprivation he fully experienced the beauty of these little flowers.

Sunday, May 28

It's only a week and a half since I began and already I feel shaky inside and terribly vulnerable. A man at church used to be a hospital orderly. He told me you can't get so personally involved or you'll burn out. I don't know how not to be personally involved.

The patients on Unit 500 live in my head. When I'm engaged in my day-to-day work I don't notice them. But as soon as my guard is down and my mind wanders, they move forward, front and center. How do men in the gay community handle learning weekly of their friends, lovers, co-workers, acquaintances testing positive for HIV, being diagnosed with AIDS, being hospitalized, dying?

One of the reasons I wanted to do this work was to help me understand what my friends in the gay community are experiencing. I don't know if I'm strong enough. I have so much to learn.

Tuesday, May 30

When I arrived at Unit 500 today the orange and white freesias were at the nurses' station. David had died the day before. "He gave up," the charge nurse told me. I looked at the orange freesias and remembered how he had cupped them in his hands and smelled their fragrance. The plants looked a little dry. I found a cup and watered them. I don't want them to die.

Several patients had been admitted since last Thursday. I noticed David's room was still vacant. I wondered if that was at the request of the nurses, like a sign of mourning. Yes, David was here. We cared for him. And now he's gone. The vacant room lets us remember that he was here and now is not.

I've felt anxious since last Thursday. When I saw Tom that day, he had just returned from a surgical procedure, implanting a Hickman catheter in his chest. That's a permanent catheter for giving nourishment and medications intravenously when it has become difficult or impossible to use veins in the arms. Tom told me his mouth felt dry and uncomfortable. I asked him if he wanted some water. He said no because of nausea. I suggested a washcloth. Yes, he would like that.

I got a fresh washcloth, moistened it and brought it to him. He carefully wiped his lips. I asked if he wanted to keep the washcloth by him. No, he didn't and handed it to me and told me to put it in the special yellow hamper for permanent disposal. I felt a moment of discomfort taking the washcloth. But it was more important to me to be there in a seemingly unafraid way than to protect myself. We talked a few minutes more and I asked if there was anything else I could do for him. Through this whole time a plastic urinal was on the sheet held upright between his knees. He asked me if I would move it to the table. I took it by the handle and carried it to the other side of the bed and put it on the table. I said goodbye and left the room. Immediately, I went to the nurses' station and washed my hands.

It was 4 o'clock and time for me to go home. I was feeling so anxious about touching the washcloth and urinal that, even though I had washed my hands, I wouldn't put my hands to my face on the drive home. And when I got home I washed carefully again. In spite of all the training about how AIDS is spread, I couldn't dislodge the anxiety. I knew in my head that the virus is only spread by exchange of body fluids, as during sex or sharing needles. Still, I couldn't shake the thought that I might have come in contact with the virus by touching that washcloth or the handle of the urinal.

Earlier in the week, a longtime volunteer at the hospital noticed me in the hallway. She saw I was wearing a volunteer badge but was in regular clothes. She asked me about myself, was I a volunteer and if so, why was I not wearing a volunteer's uniform? I told her I was a special volunteer just spending time with HIV patients on Unit 500. She told me Byrle, the unit supervisor, had called her at the volunteers' desk the week before and asked her to come to the unit and take a patient to the business office to make a financial transaction. She had told Byrle she would not enter the man's room, though she was willing to push him in a wheelchair to the business office. "I won't go into those rooms with the contamination," she had said. The anxiety I've been feeling about the washcloth and urinal make me more sympathetic about the other volunteers' fears.

When I saw Byrle coming out of his office today, I told him I needed to ask him a question. I told him about the incidents with Tom. "Should I have worn gloves to handle the washcloth and urinal?" I asked. "No, there was no danger to you," he replied and went on to say, "The rule of thumb is, if it's yucky put on gloves. The virus is fragile and dies within three or four minutes out of its nurturing environment. So, the urinal handle was safe. And as far as the washcloth goes, even casual kissing on the mouth is safe." A burden of anxiety was lifted from me.

Wednesday morning, May 31
(My daughter Ruth's 27th birthday)

The census was up yesterday. The number of HIV patients had suddenly jumped from five to eight. I felt pretty overwhelmed. I visited in every room. Most of the patients felt very sick. Most said they were nauseated and so found food unappealing. One of my jobs yesterday was to get menus marked for the next day's meals, a great job with people who are nauseated.

Bill, a new patient, an actor, couldn't do his own menu. He has severe dementia and would have forgotten what he was doing before it was done. His two daughters, both in their 20s, labored over it for me. I told them it had to be a soft diet. "How about Jello, Dad?" "No, no Jello. I don't want food." They were trying to maintain a thread from the past of how you relate to Dad. But Dad is scarcely the same now. We were taught that some dementia is common in HIV patients. But Bill's dementia is more profound than most. His daughters are struggling. They love him.

Mark was back in the hospital. I bumped into him in the hall while I was collecting menus. He had just stuck his menu in the room sign. He said, "Can you come in and talk awhile?" "Yes, I'll be right there." I was glad to see him, although I was sorry he was back so soon.

When I came into the room, he was sitting on the bed, dressed, as usual. He was wearing a white knit shirt with yellow and red piping around the neck. I noticed that it matched his Hickman catheter's red and yellow ends, which were flipped outside the neck of his shirt.

So, why was he back already I asked? He said he had had six miserable days and nights. He had had bloating in his stomach that pressed up against his diaphragm. He could only sleep two hours or so at night, then he would wake up and have to move around and sit in a chair. It was stressful. Feeling alone at night, he was anxious and fearful. The doctor readmitted him to get the bloating down and try to get his system working better. Physically he was better now that he was in the hospital. But not emotionally.

He was feeling like a terrible burden on his lover Bob. He felt Bob's high-stress work was taxing enough without him and his illness. Mark talked about a friend with AIDS who had ended his own life. Mark seemed to be turning this alternative over in his mind.

I was uncomfortable with such a serious matter. There was a little battle of identity going on inside of me. Was I Pat, the volunteer with the temporary badge? Or was I just who I am, a woman in her 50s who has had her own struggles and been laid up in hospital, and seen people die — some well, some not so well.

"Mark, I don't know what you'll need to do. But right now your work is living with AIDS. And it seems to me you've done a great job of it so far. I know from experience what it means to see someone live well, right up to the end of life. We model for each other. Bob has his own work to do and your illness may stretch him in an important way."

He was watching me closely with his beautiful light brown eyes. He was taking seriously what I was saying. The 53-year-old woman had won over the temporary badge person. Before I left, I told Mark I'd like to meet Bob some time. He looked surprised, "You haven't met Bob?" I had only met Mark briefly a week and a half before, on my first day at the hospital. But Mark is one of those people who lets you be involved in his life. It did seem as though we had known each other longer.

<hr/>

Thursday, June 1

When I arrived on Unit 500 today I checked to see who was on the floor and if the charge nurse had any directions for me. (I'm glad to say I have learned how to identify the charge nurses.) Then I went right away to see Tom. He was sitting in a chair with his lunch tray before him, every dish covered. I knocked on his open door. I wanted to announce myself since he would not have seen me enter because his head was hanging down and his eyes were closed, like he was trying to gather strength to face food. As I greeted him he belched loudly, opened his eyes, but did not lift his head. "I'm not feeling well," he said. I suggested that I could stop by later. "I don't want to push you away," he said.

I didn't know whether to stay or go. I asked him, "Are you expecting to be discharged tomorrow?" "Maybe Sunday," he said, "if that's a good discharge day." The conversation was punctuated by belches he couldn't control. They are caused by the fungus candidiasis also known as thrush in the esophagus.

Tom was sinking. Two days ago he had said he wanted it over at the hospital, didn't look forward to going home.

I wanted to make some contact while there was time. As I got up to leave, I touched his shoulder. "I want you to know I think about you." "You do?" he asked, looking up a little. Then he surprised me by asking, "Do you do a lot of speaking?" I told him no but that I was a writer and was keeping a journal of my experiences at the hospital, and that I had mentioned him several times. I hurried on to assure him that his identity was guarded, but he told me I could write about him as much as I wanted.

I told him that I am involved with gay and lesbian issues in my church. "In the church?" he asked with incredulity. "Yes, my congregation publicly welcomes gays and lesbians into full participation in the church." His head was down again, but in spite of how sick he was feeling he asked me, "What is the name of that church?" "United University Church at USC," I said, trying to imagine to what use he could put that information.

Standing, I told him that I admired him and found him courageous and gutsy. He looked up and his eyes had tears in them. I wondered if many non-gay people of my generation had given him affirmation. I left him slumped in the chair with the untouched tray before him.

Hugh has been here for at least a week but I haven't met him. The nurses have told me enigmatically that I could try speaking with him. I got the impression that he might bark at me. Each time I came to the unit I would check with his nurse and would be relieved to hear he had company or was sleeping. I did step into the room once and found him sound asleep. He's a handsome man with a mustache and Van Dyke beard.

Today I was asked to pick up Hugh's menu. I was glad for a reason to speak to him and let

14

him know I'm at the hospital. I stepped into the room and introduced myself as Pat, a volunteer, and that I was asked to pick up his menu. He hadn't barked yet. I ventured nearer to the bed and said, "I'm an APLA volunteer." That was the open sesame. He welcomed me, asked me to pull up a chair. He told me about his own volunteer work with APLA and shared some well-told anecdotes. I found him delightful, funny, and outrageous.

Friday night, June 2

I phoned the hospital and checked with the charge nurse about Tom. I mentioned that he seemed to be sinking and I asked if he was due to be discharged. She agreed that he seemed to be failing and said he might be discharged Monday. He wasn't taking phone calls Friday night. I asked her to tell him that I had called.

Monday, June 5

Over the weekend Cecil and I went hiking in the mountains with our son, Bruce, and oldest grandson, Joshua. It was wonderful to get up in the pine and fir forest of the San Jacinto Mountains.

A snatch of a melody kept running through my mind. After awhile I concentrated on it and realized that the melody was from a spiritual and went with the words "all my trials, Lord, soon be over." Tom was on my mind.

I didn't feel upset as I had at the end of my first few days of visiting in the hospital. Tom feels the suffering is worse than death. He wants to die and have the suffering ended.

Wednesday, June 7

When I got to the hospital yesterday, I found that Tom had been discharged. The lack of closure or continuity with patients is hard for me. I wanted another conversation. I wanted to be in touch. "How are you doing, Tom? How is it to be home? Is it a comfort to be with Robert? How do you like the around-the-clock nurses at your home?" But for now, at least, there is a terminus in that relationship.

I'm trying to learn how to handle these — I don't even know what to call them — "hospital friendships." I'm trying to learn how to be all there as authentically as I can for a few minutes, for a few times, and to let go of anything further. If I think there is a problem, depression, suicidal thoughts, unresolved relationships, I get in touch with the social work staff at the hospital and let them know what I've observed. Other than that, I'm trying to let go of problem solving and let go of "being there" for people in some ongoing way. It's hard.

It may be a more realistic way of living in the world, to be present as fully as possible in the moments life presents and then to let go and let the love and care we share do its own work. We can change so little in a lifetime. I'm learning some lessons in limits.

Thursday, June 8

There was an article in today's Los Angeles Times with the headline "Record Level of Violence Against Gays Reported." A record 7,248 incidents — including physical assaults, arson, vandalism and verbal abuse — had been reported to a task force by 120 churches and community and campus groups in 38 states. Seventy homosexuals had been killed in what was described as an "alarmingly widespread" pattern of violence and harassment against gay people. As I read the article I was remembering some gay friends of mine who were threatened by a car load of young bullies last year in St. Louis during our Presbyterian General Assembly. It was scary to my friends.

Of the incidents reported, 1,259, or 17 percent, were classified by local reporting groups as "AIDS-related, indicating that hatred and blame associated with the epidemic continue unabated." The article concluded with the following comments from the task force's report:

Anti-gay attacks stem from bigotry that is sanctioned and promulgated by a wide range of religious, political and social institutions … Many leaders in government, religion, entertainment and the criminal justice system have made offensive and inflammatory public comments about gay people, including statements that trivialized, legitimized and encouraged anti-gay violence.

Later in the morning I was reading my mail, which included a monthly journal being published by All Saints Episcopal Church's AIDS Service Center in Pasadena, California. The cover was a drawing by Jeffery Aldama, a 31-year-old man who recently had died of AIDS. The drawing was of his own hands as he would have spent hours looking at them while lying in the hospital bed. The drawing showed the hands and a little of the forearms. In one arm was a shunt for the IV, and the hands were fingering the IV tube like a rosary. On the other forearm was his watch.

I leafed through the magazine reading articles by persons living with AIDS (PLWAS) and by support people. Toward the end of the magazine was a piece called "Remembering Jeffery — In Precious Memory of Jeffery Aldama who passed on February 10, 1989." It was contributed by the Aldama family. It was brief and began with something Jeffery had written to his mother:

To my beautiful mother who would read me Bible stories when I was scared. You were always there. Mom, I will miss you very much from the bottom of my heart. You are my strength.

Jeffery

I couldn't continue reading the magazine because tears made it impossible to see. These are precious people. I don't want mindless violence committed against them. I want to find some way to be there for them.

A day does not pass that I do not bring up the subject of gays and lesbians with people I see, neighbors, women at my health club, friends, relatives, people at church. I'll mention a gay friend, visiting HIV patients, going to a meeting or conference on gay and lesbian issues. People are always interested and usually ask questions. It's the one thing I can do each day, tell that I'm involved with gay men and lesbian women and PLWAS (many of whom are not gay, but I think all those I've met are). I try to communicate that these connections are important to me and I count them a joy. It's something I can do to challenge the stereotypes that dehumanize and lay the groundwork that allows violence.

———◆•❋•◆———

Thursday afternoon

In the hallway of Unit 500 I saw Mark walking toward me looking jaunty. "Are you being discharged?" I asked. "No, I have shore leave for the afternoon." Then I saw his mother, Alice. We chatted a few minutes while Mark went back to get something from his room. She had seen his special diet and could hardly imagine how to prepare enough food to satisfy him given all the things he's not supposed to eat. But she seemed positive and I'll bet she'll find a way. Seeing her is like seeing an old friend, although we only met once before. Mark returned to the nurses' station where Alice and I were talking. He gave me a hug. I was touched by his affection.

Friday afternoon, June 9

Coming in at midday from running errands, there was a message on my phone machine from Debra, a social worker at APLA. She had a referral for me. "Michael is a new APLA client and expects to enter the hospital. Please stop in and see him."

Cecil is out of town today. I'm to pick him up at the airport at 8:40 p.m. After dinner I'll run out to the hospital and meet Michael before I go to the airport.

Friday evening

Michael is a young African American with an apartment near where I live. When I arrived, the nurse was in with him and he was on the phone with his mother in Michigan. I waited until he was off and asked the nurse if I'd be in the way. No, come on in.

I introduced myself to Michael as the APLA volunteer. He said he was told when he was at APLA that someone would be by to see him. This was his seventh hospitalization, all at Daniel Freeman Marina Hospital. I was startled by the number. Over what period of time I asked? Over three years. You must have been about the only HIV patient here until recently, I commented. He told me how it had been when he first was coming here.

"Everyone who came in the room had to gown up and put on mask and gloves. It made me feel pretty bad. When my friends would come it worried them, made them feel they were doing something dangerous. I knew that AIDS couldn't be communicated by casual contact, but they didn't."

"It took awhile for the hospital staff to learn that?" I asked. "Yes," he said, "but now it's different." I was standing on one side of his bed and the nurse was seated on the other side preparing to insert a shunt in his arm for the IV. Neither of us was wearing anything unusual, although the nurse wore gloves for doing the IV.

The nurse asked Michael if it was OK with him for her to go ahead while he was talking. He said yes, talking might help distract him. He explained to me that he has small, disappearing veins. The nurse began probing for a good vein. He grimaced. I put my hand on his. The nurse said, "He may need a little support through this." She got it in, but it was stinging, so she knew she hadn't gotten it in where she wanted it.

I asked Michael about what support he had from family and friends. He told me he had just been talking with his mother in Michigan, that they talk every day. She will come out to help him when he is discharged. He has a few friends out here, but he feels he can't call on them too often. And fixing meals for himself has become a problem. He's so weak. He may need to move back to Michigan to be closer to home and plans to check on medical facilities there.

I let him know I would be back Tuesday. Driving from the hospital his eyes stayed in my mind. Brown, soft, trusting. He was talking to this total stranger. But then this total stranger had made a special trip to the hospital on a Friday evening just to see him, within hours of his admittance. And she came ungowned, unmasked, ungloved and took his hand. He had reason to trust.

⋅━◦╍◦━⋅

Tuesday, June 13

We value certain parts of ourselves, and what a loss when they're gone. Over the weekend, Hugh shaved his Van Dyke beard and cut off most of his beautiful auburn hair. He looks so different, exposed. He's been having chemotherapy and chunks of his hair were coming out and his beard was getting thin. It hadn't been particularly noticeable to me. "I've always loved my hair," he said. "I don't want it to just fall out a handful at a time." So he seized the initiative, took control. But he must miss seeing that auburn hair, all thick and shiny. I do.

⋅━◦╍◦━⋅

Thursday morning, June 15

Last Tuesday there was a new patient named Ken, a charming and gentle man. Entering his room, I felt myself pull back emotionally when I saw that Ken was older, in his 60s. Most of the men I've seen have been in their 30s. It was something else I'm struggling to identify. Perhaps I am more comfortable relating to younger patients who are close to the ages of my children. In this first month I have been sorting through my wardrobe of experiences for a role to wear in these new relationships. The kind, affirming mother fits easily and is familiar. That role wouldn't work with Ken.

I liked Ken but continued to feel uncomfortable throughout our conversation of about 15 minutes. He, on the other hand, was quite revealing, although he also experienced some discomfort. But in his case he acknowledged it to me.

He described the events leading up to his being admitted to Daniel Freeman Marina Hospital. He had been feeling quite well and had planned a move from an upstairs apartment to one at street level, on the advice of his doctor. He had a moving company, actually two — one for his piano and another for the rest of the furniture. His friends and family did a lot, too, especially his brother and sister-in-law. Just sitting in a chair directing where things should go had tired him. When the china cabinet was moved, he washed the china before it went back into the cabinet.

On Sunday morning he had set out for church but became so weak he had to phone a friend to come and take him home.

When he spoke to me about the support of his friends and brother and sister-in-law, tears filled his eyes. He apologized and indicated that it embarrasses him when he cries.

I diverted my eyes and spoke words affirming tender tears as a sign of our humanity. I did not once touch him. Perhaps that's as it should be. I have thought at times that touching people may be a way of reassuring myself that we are friendly and connecting. There is a place for touching, and certainly many HIV patients want to know we are not afraid to touch them. But my own largely unconscious motives are probably liberally mixed with my needs for reassurance.

I went in to see Michael. Byrle was concerned about him and mentioned it to me. "Michael's a little depressed and he isn't having any visitors. Be sure to talk with him," Byrle had urged me as I stopped by the nurses' station.

Michael was in bed. He looked up at me with those soft brown eyes and seemed glad to see me. He said, "You mentioned you are married. Do you have children?" I could tell he had been thinking about this. I said yes, three. "Do any of them have AIDS?" he asked. No, I said. Obviously

20

he was wanting to know my motivation for this volunteer work and I tried to respond. I went into a too long, too convoluted response to Michael's curiosity. I mentioned having gay friends and getting older and finding a larger sense of family. Finally I stopped and asked if there was anything else he wanted to know about me. With a funny little smile on his face, he said no, I had already told him a lot.

After that, I moved the conversation away from me and got on to practical matters about him. When was his mother coming out? Had they found out if he has pneumonia? Michael said the doctor had done a bronchoscopy Sunday and had nicked one lung, which then collapsed. Now he was being treated for that. He said, "I'll show you." I felt hesitant about seeing whatever he was about to show me, a little embarrassment because of the intentionality.

Michael pulled the covers down to his waist and lifted his gown, revealing what looked to my untrained eye like two syringes, one about six inches long with a red plunger, the other, a bit smaller with the usual black plunger. Both were taped securely just below his diaphragm. As he showed them to me tears welled up in his eyes. I hardly knew how to respond. I asked if it made him feel like a mechanical man. He said yes, but I felt I had laid the image on him and he had said yes because it was easier.

I had noticed that his mouth and just inside his lips were chalky white. I had not mentioned it. But he brought up that his thrush was being treated and his mouth felt uncomfortable and it was a little hard to talk. I asked if the treatments were effective and he said yes.

Before I left, Michael asked me if I could find him an APLA buddy. The buddy program links up specially trained volunteers to visit and help PLWAs. I said I would check about it and let him know. I wondered if I should be encouraging him to check for himself. But I didn't mention it. Following through on patient requests restores in me a sense of control and usefulness. It's my turtle shell to keep me from feeling soft and exposed to the "predators." And what are they? The anxiety of being myself without a role? The experience of being present to suffering and unable to "help?" The knowledge of my own finitude?

Thursday evening, June 15

When I reached Ken's room, he was sitting in a chair eating lunch. I asked if he wanted me to come back or if he would like company. He invited me to sit down, although I could tell he was a little uncomfortable eating in front of me and having no food to offer me.

I felt more myself today with this older man and we had an engaging conversation, mostly about the church. He had talked about his church on the first visit, so I found out more about that. He had been raised a Lutheran in Montana but had gradually left the church because of its homophobia. For years he hadn't attended. When he moved to Southern California some friends took him to an all-gay congregation. "It felt so good to be there. Everyone was warm and friendly. And I could be myself." He had also visited a Lutheran church near his apartment, but he didn't feel at home and felt he wouldn't be accepted if they knew he was gay. "The pastor even came to visit me. And I thought about telling him I was gay. But I doubted that he would be accepting and it didn't seem worth the effort."

We were on familiar and interesting ground for both of us. We discovered we had some gay Christian friends in common. He sent his greetings to some people I would see on the weekend.

I looked in on the other two HIV patients on Unit 500. Hugh was asleep and the new patient, Blake, had a young man and woman visiting him. Across the hall Michael was getting a bath. I went to the cafeteria for a cup of coffee. While I was there Blake's two visitors came in to buy soda from a machine. I introduced myself to them and asked if Blake was a family member. The young woman answered that Blake was her brother and she introduced herself and her husband. I asked how they were doing. Her emotions were close to the surface. "It's hard. But this is Blake's second hospitalization." This was said with the sense that they were learning some things. Then she went on to say, "It's been six months since he was diagnosed and we know it's going to get worse."

Walking back to the unit I saw Hugh's parents arriving to see their son. They are from out of state. I also walked towards Hugh's room. His mother had already stepped in and, seeing Hugh asleep, sat down to read a book. It was a thick hardback and she opened it near the beginning. I admired the control she demonstrated. She seemed to anticipate a lot of waiting and was ready with something she could do. I had taken in this scene in the moment before meeting Hugh's tall, handsome, white-haired father, Bob, just outside the door to his son's room.

I said hi and he greeted me with a smile and reported, "We took the last of our children to the airport yesterday." All seven of Hugh's brothers and sisters and some spouses and at least one infant had come to see him over the weekend.

Actually there was one more to take to the airport, Hugh. His father said, "We'll be taking Hugh back with us to Baltimore. I've made arrangements for him to be admitted to the hospital there. I've been talking with Hugh's doctor here. He said that if these patients were old, they wouldn't last long with these serious cancers and other illnesses. But their hearts and lungs are young, so they can survive a lot." "How old is Hugh?" I asked. "Thirty-five."

Bob's feelings were transparent. They would pass across his face, as simple to see as storm clouds moving across the sky. Then his cheerful, good-natured, storytelling self would reappear like the clearing after a summer storm.

I meet these people, a moment in the hall, a brief conversation in a room. I watch them and I wonder about things I will never find out.

I looked in across the hall to see if Michael's mother was finished giving him a bath. I wondered what kind of relationship they had that her giving him a bath would be comfortable. Michael had told me his mother is retired. Perhaps she had been a nurse. I fleetingly tried to imagine allowing my mother to bathe me. No, I don't think that would feel comfortable to me.

I went back to the nurses' station and sat down. I was observing one of the doctors. She was wearing a flowered jersey dress and white pumps. She wore her hair loosely curled and shoulder length. She was on the phone trying to reach someone, but being put on hold every time she called. I wanted to meet her. I hadn't met any of the doctors. I felt more comfortable meeting a woman doctor. I waited around watching for when she would be off the phone.

When she finally hung up I told her who I was and she laughingly introduced herself as Dr. Murray who-kept-being-on-the-phone. I asked if she had a specialty. She said it was infectious diseases. I asked where she practiced. With a harried expression she said, "With infectious diseases you don't practice in one place. You spend all your time going from hospital to hospital. I am the primary care physician for some AIDS patients, but I consult with a lot of other physicians."

I said goodbye to Dr. Murray and bobbed down the hall again to look in on Michael. His mother was washing her hands at the sink next to the door. She saw me hesitating because Michael was snoozing sitting up in the chair. I wondered if he wanted to be back in bed.

His mother is a short, powerful looking woman, compact, with light brown skin like her son's. She's no-nonsense and signaled to me to come in. "He's been nodding off like that all day," she said. And her tone indicated that she thought he needed to stay awake more and that a visitor might help. I went in and sat on the other chair opposite Michael. His mother's conversation had roused him a little.

"Hi, Michael. I wanted to stop by to see how you're doing," I said. His eyes began to droop again. It looked like medication-induced sleep. I tried to be more lively and engaging so I wouldn't fail his mother, but also because I had something I wanted to find out from him. In a more animated voice I commented on his mother being there, remembering how much he had looked forward to her arrival, like a hope for health or an expectation that suffering might end with her arrival.

I asked if the equipment which had been taped to his chest had been removed. He looked up at me with those trusting eyes. He opened the lapels of his robe to show me his bare and hairless chest. The syringes were gone. I was happy for him. That ordeal was over. His eyelids slid shut again.

I asked when he would be discharged. His mother said it would be over the weekend. I asked Michael if anyone had phoned him about a buddy. He nodded no. I didn't feel confident that he was tracking the conversation or would remember in his drowsiness if someone from APLA had called. There was no point in trying to continue. I told his mother that I was glad to have met her and that I had enjoyed getting acquainted with her son, and left.

Stopping by Hugh's room, I looked in to see if he was still asleep. Hugh always has a clutter of things on the moveable table next to his bed, making it hard to see him. But his mother, Esther, smiled and signaled me in. Hugh was awake and had been visiting with his parents, who were seated in two of the three chairs in that room. I stood by the bed, unsure if I should join the conversation or only stop by.

I asked Hugh when he would be discharged. He said it would be Monday, and that he would be flying home to Baltimore. He had some exciting plans which he started describing with his characteristic personal power. It was not a kind of manic grabbing on to something to deny his illness. It seemed to me to come out of his strength, a brilliant young man with visions, who would live until he died.

He had figured out some things to sell, principally his motorcycle, so he could buy a computer. But the plan he was most excited about was getting funding for Mothers of AIDS Patients (MAP), a loose, national affiliation of mothers. Hugh went on to say that mothers run up huge phone bills talking to their sick children and calling doctors and trying to get information. He wanted to go after grants from ARCO and AT&T for the national organization to make available to mothers who needed help with their phone bills. He also wanted to have enough money for MAP to strengthen work out of their central office. He felt that mothers of AIDS patients love their children so much that they could help turn around not only fear of AIDS but also homophobia itself. He especially mentioned having an impact on homophobia in the church. Glancing at Esther's strong, open, intelligent face, I thought he might be right. I pulled up the third chair in the room and sat down to hear his plans.

When I came to the hospital today, I had on my agenda that I wanted to tell Hugh that I'm

24

a writer. On our first visit he had talked about writing and I would have mentioned it then, but we were interrupted by some medical procedure. Since then he had had all this company. It felt important to me to tell him, especially to tell him that I'm writing a journal from my hospital experiences. Hugh strikes me as the kind of person who would want to know that I was writing about persons with AIDS in the hospital and might not like to find out later that I was writing about him and others without his knowledge, even if their identities were concealed. He seemed interested when I told him. I asked Hugh to tell me more about his writing. He explained that during his illness he had written four articles and all had been published. He sat up and reached beside his bed and brought up his briefcase. I was surprised that he had a briefcase with him. He fingered through file folders looking for a particular article, but didn't find it. He did, however, pull out a poem he had written. He handed it to me to read. I had a little trepidation that I might not understand it. I concentrated, drawing myself in to focus only on that 8½-by-11-inch sheet of white paper with Hugh's thoughts and feelings represented by words on the page. It was about being sick and at home again. He had probably written it when he first left Los Angeles and returned home to Baltimore. It revealed some of the complicated feelings we are apt to have in returning home as adults in a rather passive state.

Hugh continued talking about writing and his plans to write using the new computer. I said that it sounded healthy. His father, sitting next to me and quiet through all this conversation, was suddenly animated and said, "He is healthy."

His affirmation of Hugh was a little explosion of feeling.

I told Hugh that I had had three major surgeries in a recent two-year period. I had been writing a book during the first two surgeries, and the writing had kept me going, helped me to define myself as a person who writes and has work to do, not a patient. He asked me if I had had cancer. I was embarrassed to say that none of the surgeries was disease related. Embarrassed because these surgeries, the two orthopedic and the hysterectomy, suddenly seemed trivial in the face of his condition. I wished I had not mentioned them.

I was uncomfortable with what I had shared and decided it was time to leave and let them return to private conversation. I felt a little sad that I probably would not see Hugh or his parents again. Our lives had intersected and now would diverge. I told Hugh that I had liked getting acquainted and I meant it. With goodbyes all around, I went out into the hall and down to the nurses' station to check in with the charge nurse before I left for the day.

Tuesday, June 20

There were new patients on the unit today. A man named Roy was in for the day on an outpatient basis having a blood transfusion. He was not in a room on the long 500 corridor but in a room on the hall that makes a T with that corridor. The rooms on that hall are quiet and away from some of the bustle. I went in and met Roy. This was his fourth transfusion. He had not had a regular admittance to the hospital and looked healthy with his reddish blond hair and pink cheeks. He is an average size man, probably in his mid-30s. He was watching TV to pass the time while the blood slowly entered his veins. At the end of our brief conversation he told me his doctor wants to admit him for tests. I felt he dreaded the possibility.

The nurses' station is where the T is crossed. As I came out of Roy's room I was surprised and glad to see Hugh's mother walking by the nurses' station. "So, you all haven't left yet?" I said. "No, they plan now to discharge Hugh tomorrow and we're going to fly him home to Baltimore. He'll go right into the hospital when we get there." She went on to say that Hugh was going downhill, that they had seen quite a change since they had been in Los Angeles. "I didn't want to see him make the trip out here. One of his legs was quite swollen before he left Baltimore. That's from the K.S. [Kaposi's sarcoma, a tumor of the walls of the blood vessels. On internal organs it can be fatal.] But he's an adult. What could I say? I told him I didn't think it was a good idea. But he missed his friends and the things he was active in here. And he had some business he wanted to take care of. He was staying with my sister while he was out here. He was planning to drive up the coast and my sister said, 'Hugh, I'm concerned about that leg. Let me see it.' He took his pants off and the leg was huge. She just told him, 'We're calling the doctor and taking you to the hospital right now.' That's when he came in here."

Standing by the nurses' station, we were two women in our 50s. Two women who have borne children and did a good job of raising them. But later in life learned about homosexuality in a way that had sunk in. She went on to tell me in a low, quiet voice that Hugh had been 27 before they learned that he was gay. "I don't know where I had been that I didn't realize it before. I wish we had been there for Hugh when he was trying to find himself as a gay man." I watched her face as she talked. She kept her emotions to herself, but I knew she expressed the authenticity of her feelings in action. When I first met her she had said, "Oh, I want to talk to you about what you do. I want to do something like hospital visitation back home in Baltimore."

She mentioned that intention again as we stood by the nurses' station.

She and her husband were 100 percent there for Hugh now, without sentimentality, just solid, practical, dependable, and sacrificial, in the way that we sacrifice for our children and it doesn't seem like any sacrifice at all.

A man named Jimmy was back in the hospital. He had been out about two weeks. His mother, Ruth, was always with him. Now she was sitting at the end of the bed, gently massaging his legs. He looked much worse. His gorgeous blue eyes were completely round like two portholes in a ship and the ship was ravaged. He had been thin before. He was much thinner now. They were waiting for a CAT scan to be taken. He had been telling the doctor for six months that he had a growth on the left side near his stomach. The doctor had never been able to find it. Now it was protruding. He showed me his side. The growth beneath the skin was visible. It was nearly 2 in the afternoon and I commented that I supposed he had not been able to eat or drink in preparation for the CAT scan. He said it didn't matter, he didn't eat anything anyway. He rested his head back on the pillow and grimaced.

I asked Ruth, "Have you been home at all since you were last here?" "No, I've just stayed with him. My house is just three blocks from Jimmy's, but I've scarcely been home. I just want to be with him." Jimmy said, "And I'm glad she does."

David, a journalist, was admitted yesterday. The charge nurse said he had been in the hospital once before. She felt for him. "He's always been an active person. The opportunistic virus he has has paralyzed his legs. He's having a hard time of it."

When I looked into the room I saw an Episcopal priest who looked familiar. He remembered me from the 1970s when he had been in campus ministry and I had worked at the edge of the University of Southern California campus. He was kind to tell me his name, Reverend Duncan. "David here is one of our parishioners," he said. Standing at the foot of the bed, I greeted David. He was a handsome Hispanic man with a straight mustache which accentuated a wide mouth and very even white teeth. I introduced myself as the APLA volunteer at this hospital. He grinned, in fact laughed, as though I had told him a wonderful piece of news. Surprised, I asked him the meaning of his response. His face changed. "I'm just so honored," he said. He began to cry. I moved past Reverend Duncan to stand next to David. "You're a mom aren't you?" he said in a squeaky, emotion-laden voice. "Yes."

"Do you have kids?" he asked, looking at me and crying a little. "Yes, I do." I stroked his arm, not knowing what to make of all this emotion. I told him I would come back later to see him.

I was shaken by his outburst of feeling. I stood around in the hallway hoping to catch Alicia, the charge nurse that day, not because she was in charge but because I like her a lot and just wanted, needed, to tell someone what had happened. I was close to tears myself. Alicia came out of a patient's room and I related what had happened. Her eyes were wide with surprise and curiosity about the outburst.

I made a few notes in a little notebook I carry when I'm at the hospital. Usually the brief notes are to remind me of who I've seen and a fact or two I don't want to forget. For David I put down, "I'm so honored." "You're a mom," which had been more a statement than a question. I wouldn't need these notes to jog my memory. Rather, I think they served to get the startling experience objectified out there on paper.

Later, I learned from his nurse that David has some neurological complications that may have caused his surprising display of emotion.

Ina, from the dietician's office, saw me in the hallway and in her wonderful Scottish brogue explained about all the menus she hadn't been able to get from the guys for the next day. Hugh's was one of them. He had been sleeping, but I told her I would slip in and try to find it. I tiptoed into the room but that wasn't necessary. He was awake. He looked calm. He's a man who doesn't like it when people scurry around anxiously. And he wouldn't usually expend himself on fretting. However, when I asked him how he felt about the anticipated flight to Baltimore, he said, "I'm anxious about it." He also was concerned about all the money his parents had spent to get the family to Los Angeles to see him and now to fly him first class, with medical equipment and maybe a nurse, to get him home.

Can anyone who has not had children understand how little of a sacrifice it is to do whatever your children need? I know not all parents are generous with their children. Yet, I believe it is in the natural order of things to do anything our children need, anything in our power.

I encouraged Hugh to rest his mind about this since his parents seemed to be doing what they wanted to do. Didn't he feel they wanted to do what they were doing? He acceded that it seemed so.

In the quiet of Hugh's darkened room, with only a little light slipping in between the slats of the blinds, we said goodbye again. I told him that I was finding it difficult to meet people I like and then to let them go. He had a calm smile on his face and said, "Yes, I expect it is a difficult discipline." I spoke truthfully. But he spoke out of a more profound understanding of that experience. He soon would let go of all of us and of everything he has known.

He extricated his right hand from under the covers. It looked as though it was heavy, weighted down by the shunt and tubing. He lifted it to meet mine.

Going out of the room and down the hall to the nurses' station I was preparing to leave for home. Seeing Byrle, I stopped to talk for a few minutes. We stepped into his office just up the hall that crosses the T. A couple of minutes later through the office door I saw Robert, Tom's lover, walking toward the nurses' station. I hailed him. He asked me if I'd seen Tom. No, was he in the hospital? Yes, in the Intensive Care Unit. Where is that I asked him? He didn't know and had come to familiar old Unit 500 to find out.

Byrle, with a sense of efficient urgency, said he would walk with us to ICU. He would have to take us in. Hurrying through the corridor toward the center of the hospital, Byrle strode in front of us. "When did Tom come into the hospital?" I asked Robert. "Yesterday," he said. "He's dying." His voice cracked with emotion. I reached out and stroked his shoulder as we hurried along. "How are you? Do you have support people?" "Yes, I have lots of friends," he smiled. "How about Tom's father. Has there been contact?" I asked. "Yes, they talked on the phone." "Was there some reconciliation, Robert?" "Yes, there was."

We reached the double doors for ICU opening off the hallway to our right. Byrle swept us into a restricted corridor for a short distance. At the door to ICU he told us to wait. He stepped in and found which cubicle Tom was in and then returned to direct us. I wondered if we would have to put on gowns or masks. Everything was so quick I scarcely had time to look around. Tom was in the nearest cubicle.

Tom, a gnarled head muzzled with a blue oxygen mask. A rasping, frantic sound of breathing. Where was his body? There was scarcely a shape visible under the sheet. It was as though his body had disappeared and left only his head. I moved closer, Robert on his right and I on his left. I could see a little of his anguished face above the mask. He spoke to Robert with urgency. First a status report. "They are trying to regulate my breathing." Then, "Did you speak to my father?" Robert responded yes. "Did you talk about the insurance?" I missed Robert's response, so overwhelmed was I by what I was experiencing. Tom's face had been turned toward me as he spoke to Robert as though it would take too much precious energy to both turn and speak. Without lifting his head he raised his eyes. "Is it Kay?" he asked me, making an effort to remember my name. "Pat, that's all right," I reassured him.

"I need a towel," Tom said with urgency. "And I need it now." Byrle was at the end of the bed and grabbed a towel from a table I had not noticed. "I need it under me." Byrle deftly smoothed the towel under him managing to keep Tom's emaciated body covered. I was impressed with the control and dignity Tom was able to manage under the circumstances.

Robert was caressing Tom's arms as they lay under the cover, just as I had seen him do the first time I met them. I found Tom's shoulder to touch it. Then in a wave of feeling I stroked his brow.

Tom was not the kind of man to invite such a show of affection, but it was so near the end. "Dear friend," I said to him and tears seemed to well up in his eyes. "I'm not going to stay." So much was happening and Tom had urgent matters to settle with Robert. I felt out of place. I started for the door but saw Robert break into tears and turn away from Tom. So Tom wouldn't see? I went around the bed and embraced Robert, kissed his face.

I didn't see Byrle as I went through the door, although he must have been standing right there. I wasn't crying. I simply did not have the capacity to take in anything else. Then I saw that Byrle was right behind me, leaving with me. We went through the door and down the corridor toward the double doors. A group of nurses in surgical green were coming onto the corridor. That must be a surgery room.

When we got through the double doors Byrle told me what he was going to do. What he said didn't entirely register and I was surprised that he would be telling me. I couldn't think of why. Maybe there was a reason. Maybe he was upset too and this was a way to get closure on the experience we had just had together.

I got my car from the parking lot and drove onto the freeway for my short ride home. I was unsettled. Should I have stayed in the room? Should I have told Robert I would be waiting some place if he needed consolation? Should I have found a place and maintained a vigil to honor the ending hours of a man's life? I didn't know. By the time I arrived home I was able simply to acknowledge that I didn't know what I should have done and decided to speak to someone with more experience. Different possibilities ran through my mind. I phoned Byrle. "Byrle, this is Pat. I didn't know what to do, whether to stay or go." He reassured me, "What you did was exactly right, very appropriate. It was your first time with someone sick in ICU. There was a lot going on. Tom had things to take care of with Robert. You did the right thing."

⚬⟶⬩⟵⚬

Friday, June 23

Yesterday, late in the afternoon, Mark was unexpectedly readmitted. This was his third hospitalization in the month I've been at the hospital. When I went into his room he was bent over, removing his shoes. I asked why he was back so soon. As he told me about the nausea he was experiencing from the medication, tears welled up in his eyes.

30

Mark had impressed me, during his two previous stays in the hospital, with the ways he maintained his identity. He was always dressed in his own clothes, soft, comfortable leisure wear. He would be out of bed sitting in the recliner in his room. He read the paper in the morning. In the afternoon his mother, Alice, would come to the hospital with Arlo, his dog. They could visit in the patio.

He has worked hard at being Mark, at continuing some normal life, at not giving up to AIDS. But it's a terrible illness, and on this afternoon Mark's spirit seemed bent over as he removed his shoes and swung himself into the bed, fully clothed. My heart went out to him. But how to express that?

I touched his shoulder and told him I was sorry. "You can't be sorry," he responded with irritation, not looking at me. There is a fine line between receiving another person's sorrow, allowing its expression, and weighing that person down with your own long face. I think I missed this time and added an ounce to Mark's already weighted balance of suffering.

I felt a bond with Mark. My own hope had been increased by his stubborn hold on life lived in his own clothes. I have struggled with maintaining identity and some sense of personal control when I have been sick and in the hospital. Mark has done this so well. I wanted him to hold on to that which also gave me hope. I wanted to encourage Mark, perhaps for my own sake.

That night after dinner I drove to a flower shop that I knew would still be open. On the way I composed a message for the card. I kept trying it out in my mind. Do I feel comfortable with this message? How will Mark receive this message? To the first question, my answer was that I was a little uncomfortable. There was some risk, some reaching across the chasm which divides us all from one another. I wanted to throw across a line of hope and I was shaping my rope from nothing more than intuition.

I bought yellow tiger lilies and wrote the brief message on a small blank card with Conroy Florists embossed on the cover.

Take heart, Mark. All the power of love and goodness is on your side. Pat

I then drove to the hospital, walking in the back door again, pinning on my volunteer badge. Coming on Unit 500, it was rather quiet. At the end of the hall I could see that Mark's door was closed. There was subdued visiting in several patient rooms. I knocked on Mark's door and cracked it open a little and called his name. He invited me in.

He was feeling comfortable now, was sitting up in bed with a pillow behind his head and was wearing his own clothes, as usual. This time he was wearing a soft, oversized flannel shirt in a blue and gray plaid. I set the bud vase with the yellow tiger lilies on the overbed table next to him. He smiled looking at them.

"They are the color of my first car," he said and began to describe not only his first car but a second one which was red. "You seem very interested in cars," I said. "It's one of my passions," he replied, and a moment of sorrow passed across his face. His passion for cars was just one of the things that would be ending.

"I brought you a card. It's not fancy." I handed him the little card. He read it and tears filled his eyes. A drop overflowed and ran down toward the pillow.

We visited quietly for an hour. He talked about growing up Catholic, going to college with Mormons in Salt Lake City, and his determination to affirm who he was, a gay man. He talked about turning away from religion that made a person feel shame for who he is. "I knew the only gift I had to give was the person God made me to be. I'm no longer involved in religion, but I have my own spirituality."

He told me about his niece and nephew and sister. He felt a special concern for and bond with his nephew. The children's father had abandoned the family. Uncle Mark was a special person for his nephew. The boy and Mark knew that his illness meant another kind of desertion. As Mark talked about it, he stopped in mid-thought. He felt a responsibility to the boy and he was leaving him. Mark didn't have to say it. The thought was visible on his face.

I asked him how he had met Bob. A little smile appeared. His eyes were focused toward the corner of the ceiling as he saw in memory the party where they met, the beautiful Italian man he had been watching, his hope of meeting him when the Italian had moved into the hall and Mark had followed, but too late. Then Bob had stepped out, "How am I so lucky to find you out here alone?" he had asked.

"How romantic," I commented. "Yes, he's a romantic guy," and tears came again but did not overflow. All these losses to anticipate!

He asked me why I had chosen to do this work of visiting HIV patients. I told him about my gay friend Chris and his pain at the suffering of his friends and colleagues. I wasn't able to give him a sensible explanation to his question, although he seemed satisfied with my impressionistic stream of consciousness. Or, perhaps, with a tear or two which came when I spoke of my friend's pain.

Perhaps in reflecting on our visit I have begun to unravel for myself the reason I'm doing this work. I need the closeness, the sense of shared humanity. I encourage them in their struggle because I need encouragement. Can Mark understand the hope I feel from his courage to go on living his life in the face of AIDS?

———————

Tuesday, June 27

This afternoon was uneventful for me on Unit 500. Many dramas were taking place and it was busy, but there wasn't much for me to do. But I did what I could and have to trust that it was of some small value to others. We feel best about ourselves when we feel valued and purposeful. In both categories I felt a little shaky this afternoon. The staff was frazzled and two of them were short-tempered with me when I asked a question about a patient. Usually friendly, accessible Dr. Murray had been direct, "I don't have time to talk. I'm having a terrible day." I saw myself with my cheap volunteer badge and felt ashamed to have interrupted critical work.

I spent some uncomfortable time with David, the journalist, getting him to fill out his menu requests for tomorrow. Apparently because of the neurological damage, his thoughts ramble. Last week when we did his menu, I told him each group of choices and he told me what to mark. That had been a positive experience. The menu task was focused and objective, and David had been able to stay rooted in reality. No such luck today. He wanted to mark it himself; I told him I would wait while he made his choices.

It took a long time. I tried to limit his conversational diversions and keep him focused on the menu. When he was finally done, it was useless. He had put big circles around almost all categories, like every juice offered for breakfast. I went back to the dietician's office and marked another one with the things he told me previously that he liked.

There were seven HIV patients on the unit. I prowled the hall looking for something useful to do. One patient was sleeping, another was out of his room for a surgical procedure, another spoke Spanish and I didn't trust my limited vocabulary. I spent a few minutes with Bill, the older patient with advanced dementia.

I spent time with Mark. He was the only patient who wanted to visit. Mark is once again in the room at the end of the hall with a window facing onto the patio where we first met and where the dog can visit. He talked about noise. He was complaining about the hospital gardener using power equipment to cut and edge the grass just outside his window. Now that it is summer patients often have their windows open. Mark expresses a deep longing for quiet.

During the conversation I felt strangely inept. I've spent quite a bit of time with Mark. I don't know how to have a prolonged "hospital friendship." Do I share something of myself? Do I let him know how he has touched me? I'm not sure of the boundaries.

Thursday, June 29

Sylvester was a little hard to look at. His lips had been raw, open bleeding sores. Now they were crusted over and still bleeding. A single trail of bright red blood had run down his chin but he did not know it. While we talked he dabbed at his lips and chin with tissues. He talked about getting out of the hospital and eating right and getting better. "How is your appetite, Sylvester?" "Not very good."

David, the journalist, has original art leaning on the furniture around his room and there are always flowers, from people's gardens. He's a classy guy. He has continued to be very emotional. But today he calmly showed me his handkerchief. "This one is soiled," he said, although it looked quite fresh. "That one over there in the box," he said pointing me to a vinyl box which had held two new handkerchiefs. "Take that one in case you meet someone who cries. You do see people who cry?" he asked. "Yes, and sometimes it's me," I responded.

This afternoon I had gone first to see Mark. Two nurses had said to be sure to see him because he was depressed. His room was dark and Mark was in bed with the covers up to his chin. He said he was glad to see me, that he was having a rotten day. He had just started telling me all that had happened when an attendant arrived to take him for a chest X-ray. "I'll only be a few minutes. Will you come back to see me?" His request bypassed my head and reached my heart. It was not his need which affected me but his desire to open to me his experience and, on this day, his sadness. I told him I would watch for him.

When he returned from X-ray, one of the doctors was ready to see him. He was tied up the rest of the afternoon. When I was ready to leave for the afternoon, I asked his nurse to tell him I would come back after dinner to see him.

We finally had our conversation in the evening. Mark had the back of his bed up for sitting. He described the events of the last 24 hours, especially the inconclusive results of a biopsy of a sore on his arm. It might be Kaposi's sarcoma. In a quiet, reflective voice he said, "I guess this thing is going to unfold tear by tear."

His lover arrived and we met for the first time. An upbeat kind of guy, handsome, with a pixieish sense of humor. He arrived outside the window of Mark's first-floor room, slipping between the building and a concrete block baffle and through the shrubbery to let Mark see his dog. I recognized Bob from his picture, but seeing me, he thought he had the wrong room and scooted away. When he came in the room we met each other. He was holding a clipboard and asked if I would sign a petition asking the state legislature to place an initiative on the ballot for increased AIDS funding. I kept busy signing it while Bob and Mark tenderly greeted each other. It felt like it was time to leave. I took Mark's hand to say goodbye. He asked me if I would be back tomorrow. No, I wouldn't. I felt a pull. Couldn't I set aside whatever work I planned to do tomorrow and be here? I have a hard time setting limits. My inclination is to turn myself over to friends and loved ones if they ask for me. "I'll phone you tomorrow, Mark," I said.

❖

Friday, June 30

I have other work to do, and I haven't been able to get myself detached from the patients at the hospital. Unlike Tuesday, yesterday afternoon was rewarding. I had satisfying exchanges with a couple of patients and with some family members. One of the doctors asked for my help with a patient's family. And the psychologist at the hospital gave me some good feedback from patients about my visits with them. I've nearly forgotten how inept I felt Tuesday. How easily I succumb to a passing feeling of being important to someone else, and how easily that sense of value can evaporate, like a lovely cologne that is squirted on and in a little while the essence is gone.

❖

An Addition for June 30

Tom died at 7:08 p.m.
This afternoon I had phoned the nurses' station to ask about him. The nurse told me that Tom had been released from ICU late the day before and brought to Unit 500. She said he was not good. He had had some lucidity in the morning, but then in the afternoon nothing seemed to register. I had thought about going over for a few minutes, but I didn't.

Later his nurse told me about the end. His lover, Robert, had been with him. I could picture Robert caressing Tom's arms as they lay beneath the blanket, as I had seen him do at other times, and quietly waiting. Four years of love and sharing ended. And what will lie ahead for Robert?

❖

Sunday, July 2

I stopped in to see David this afternoon. His room was full of attractive women. I asked how he rated so many beautiful women in his room. Two were aunts and two were nieces. They seemed to be having a good time with David. He is charming and funny. But his lightness and joking can turn instantly to pathos.

David gives me gifts. The other day it was the man's handkerchief, in case I met someone who cries. This day, lying in the bed, his legs still paralyzed, he reached for a picture postcard. It was an impressionistic painting of a man with a calla lily and leaf by his heart. This was another rendering of a piece of original art there in David's room. In that one the man has a golden heart. "This is the same artist, David. Was he your lover?" He didn't have to say, it was so clear. We all thought David eccentric having all these paintings leaning on the furniture around his room. And because of the neurological damage, I had not wanted to ask him why he had them there, anticipating a torrent of loose associations. He had surrounded himself with memories of his lover, Michael, who had died of AIDS. The paintings kept Michael close through David's own ordeal. And now he was giving me this picture by Michael. It was the head and shoulders of a man, unadorned, without hair or clothing, a benign smile on a calm, uncomplicated face. And a lily and green leaf at his heart. A painting of goodness. David turned it over and with effort wrote, "With love." He did not sign his name. Perhaps the painting had been done with love and he now gave it to me with love. Unsigned, it was like a symbol that it was from both David and Michael.

Tuesday, July 4
(It's my birthday tomorrow.)

The other day I went in to see a patient who had been admitted the day before. The new patient, Eddie, was in bed lying on his side with his back toward the door. He was talking with a woman friend who was seated in a chair next to the bed. I knocked on the open door and called his name. Stepping into the room, I introduced myself as I took in the scene. Eddie turned his head toward me. He was skinny and looked like he might have always been skinny. His face had a pitiful expression. All he said was, "I want to get out of here," as though anyone who walked through the door might be able to release him.

I told my husband this story and he said, "Oh, like you after your knee surgery." It was painful to remember that I had been so pitiful. I defended myself by telling him, "But I would not have said that to strangers."

Sylvester has a different response to the hospital. The other day he told me he would be in for another week and said that he wasn't anxious to go home. "I'm getting stronger here." I told him about the lounge opening onto the patio. He was pleased to know he could walk to an outdoor spot and carefully reviewed the directions. "I go down the hall to the nurses' station, turn left, go into the lounge on my left and onto the patio." His face was animated as he anticipated doing things and getting stronger in the hospital.

Mark thought he might be discharged soon, but he was in no hurry. "I don't want to take responsibility for all these meds," he told me referring to his medication.

Sitting at the nurses' station, a young nurse named Phyllis told me, "Some of the patients like to be here because they feel safe with all the nurses around."

I expect that's true. Several of the patients have told me of frightening experiences they have had at home when unexpected things happened in their bodies: inability to sleep, bloating, vomiting, paralysis. They were rushed to the hospital, and under the doctor's orders, the nurses gently got them more comfortable. I've observed some of the nurses on this unit with their patients. They have been cheerful, kind, and hopeful with a hope based on limited, short-term goals. "We'll get you more comfortable in a few minutes ... This will let you sleep ... Here is something for your nausea."

Of course the hospital provides its own frightening experiences. Some of the high-tech "procedures" are frightening and painful. Patients speak about probes and visualizing equipment inserted into orifices in their bodies, or having to lie in one uncomfortable position in a small chamber. And lack of control or sense of participation can be frightening. Mark was awakened at midnight by nurses in his room starting a medicine intravenously into a blood vessel near his heart through the Hickman, the surgically implanted intervenous catheter. "What's going on? What are you giving me?" It was Dilantan. Something about the dose or taking it on an empty stomach caused strange and terrible reactions in his body. He said it was worse than any drug trip he had had while a student in the 1960s.

37

Friday, July 7

I don't remember much poetry. Lines I do remember are apt to have significance for me. Yesterday I was remembering a line from John Milton's poem on his blindness: "They also serve who only stand and wait." I sit and wait with the patients. They sit and wait for the next thing to happen, the medicine to come, a procedure to be done, the doctor to stop by, a discharge order to come, or death. I need to know that identity and value remain intact when my active life becomes inactive. Many of the patients have the same questions about who they are and what continuing purpose they have. We are examining these things, if not together, in tandem.

Yesterday the nurse told me Mark didn't feel like talking. I went in just to check. He was lying on his stomach. "Mark, are you sleeping? I can come back." "No, come in. I'm glad to see you." As he turned over, something was triggered on his IV pole and the beeper went off. He called for the nurse and angrily ordered the pole removed from his room. He wanted an ordinary pole without a beeper. These special poles are used to signal the nurse when it's time to change a bag of medication or fluid. They're helpful to the nurses but often irritating to the patients, especially because the poles beep mistakenly.

Mark was in a dark, angry mood. I was grateful he wasn't angry with me. For 30 or 40 minutes I sat and listened, commenting occasionally, but mostly listening. He had a lot on his mind. The doctors had discovered a parasite in his body. He had the same parasite last year and nearly died from the associated fevers. It's one of the most difficult parasites to kill, he said. Also they had diagnosed herpes all through his throat. His left arm was still extremely sore where a growth was removed last week. It's infected, probably with herpes. His lover has had the flu. Friends who had visited had not seemed helpful or comforting. They felt compelled to do something. I knew how they must feel. I've been a compulsive fixer most of my life.

I sat and listened. Then I said I would be going. "Would you like a hug, Mark?" "I sure would." We hugged and then he said, "Today started out rotten, but it's getting better." That made me feel marvelous. What a lovely thing to say.

It's hard to believe that our best gift might be to sit and wait, through the pauses when nothing is said, through the anger, and sometimes through the abrupt responses. All my life I have believed that the mark of caring was the willingness to do something, to take action, to be an advocate. Now I see that there is also a place for caring of another kind. A tree does nothing, but we love its shade. We can stretch out our arms like leafy branches and bring coolness and shade in the desert.

Sunday, July 9

A week ago another man named David was admitted. I'll call him Nurse David. I met him when he arrived. He does home care nursing with AIDS patients and is committed to his work. He is himself HIV-infected. He came to the hospital directly from a patient's home. David had been nauseated and vomiting for three days. At the hospital he stayed on his feet much of the time, was dressed in a tank top and running shorts. He had obtained passes twice from his doctor to walk to the adjacent shopping center, the first time to shop for his 31st birthday, which he spent in the hospital. The second pass was for last Thursday afternoon to go to see the Indiana Jones movie, *Raiders of the Lost Ark*. At 4 o'clock, when I was about to leave the hospital, he returned and was standing at the nurses' station asking his nurse for treatment for severe pain in his back and neck from a recent car accident. I watched this tall, young man in his bright colored tank top and shorts, his tall body straight and at one time, I'm sure, strong to help. He was trying to hold back his tears as he got the response that every patient has gotten at some time, "The doctor hasn't left an order for that, but I'll see what I can do."

I watched David go down the hall to his room and followed him. He was sitting on the edge of the bed with his head down. I went over to where he was sitting and started to gently stroke his painful neck and shoulders and noticed his beautiful curly hair, well groomed and long enough in back for the curls to show. He straightened up like a ramrod, his mouth a hard line, "I don't want pity." "I'm not giving you pity, David." I stayed with him for half an hour or more while he sent off angry sparks. He alternated between angry expressions and tears. He was the caregiver, unaccustomed to needing help. It made him feel weak. He couldn't recognize himself. He has a battle mentality and a determination to beat AIDS. Before I left he let me take his hand. We talked about the new challenge of getting strength and energy from others. I asked if he would like a hug. He said yes he would.

When I left and walked by the nurses' station, his nurse, a person very much like him, was fuming about what a pain in the ass David was. It's easier to be a volunteer than a nurse.

I got my permanent badge today. My name in green letters.

———— ◆•••◆ ————

Monday, July 10

This afternoon I phoned Mark to ask if he would like to go on a short outing to a nearby park when I visit tomorrow. I was calling ahead since an outing would require a pass from his doctor. Mark's voice sounded terrible. When I placed the call I was on a track of my own making. Hearing his voice I stopped. He wasn't able right now to get on my track. I wanted to get on his. "What's happening, Mark?" "I can't tell you on the phone. Can you come over?" he asked.

Driving over, there were all these thoughts. Was he being manipulative with me? Was I once again copping out on my work? I had just finished writing a funding proposal for a non-profit organization and wanted to write the cover letter and get it ready to mail. As I swung onto the freeway for the short distance to the hospital, I relaxed and said to myself that I had been working at the computer all day and had done good work. This man is very sick and wants to see me. I want to respond now. So just move into this experience and let it unfold.

Mark looked terrible, probably hadn't shaved for two days.

He was holding a foot-high bear lent to him by his friend, Carol. He insisted I hold it, and no, I had to turn it around facing me. What is this about? Holding the bear to me I heard and felt its heartbeat. Like your mother, like your lover, like your dog lying next to you comfortingly alive, heart beating and warm. Mark, what is happening? He formed his words slowly, sadly, tears as slowly rolling down his cheeks. I leaned close to hear. "It's time to let go," he said. He went on to softly say that he had talked with Bob, with Carol, with his sister and mother and it was OK with them.

Now, he turned to me and asked if it was OK with me. Inside my head I'm saying, "God damn no, it's not OK with me." But I'm thinking what right do I have to refuse permission if all these others have said yes. And I can't even yet think of why he is asking me. What has happened? Why now?

I ask him questions and he gives me answers. He is not thinking of suicide because of what it would do to others. He feels he has said goodbye to all the people he cares most deeply about. The last one was his closest friend who with his wife and child had visited on the weekend, had made a long journey to be with him. I asked about the child, his dear friend's 2-year-old son, long sought and much loved. Mark reached to the bedside table and got a snapshot of the boy, showed it to me. I asked the child's name and he told me, but my own tears have washed it away. But his little face and bright blue eyes are in my mind. I handed the photo back to Mark. He gazed with a sad sweetness at this representation of the very seed of his dear friend.

He said there was nothing left he wanted to do. He would enjoy having as much conversation with me as I had time for. And he wanted to spend as much time as he could with Bob. He did not want to die at home because home and their bed would then always remind Bob of that loss.

I was crying a little but trying not to get lost in my feelings. If he had nothing left he wished to do, why should he not die? But I was not ready to give my permission, for whatever that might be worth. Such a surprising request. I told him I had to go and that I would be back tomorrow and we would go to the park if he wanted. I would be there at 1 p.m. and for him to think of what he wanted to tell me about himself. I wanted him to plan for the future, even if it was only tomorrow and a brief visit to the park, or perhaps a further revelation of something of himself.

❧

Wednesday, July 12

Mark was not well enough to go to the park. We talked for a little while, he so quietly I strained to hear. He had no tears today. It was like a quiet resignation. He has always liked conversation, but he did little initiating today. I had things on my mind I wished to ask about and did.

Why had he gone from his home in San Francisco to college in Salt Lake City? Without lifting his hand he directed my eyes with his to the class ring on the ring finger of his right hand. I had noticed it before, a gold ring with a large red stone. He apparently wanted me to read the inscription but I couldn't. He took the ring off and handed it to me. It said State University of Utah. "It was my father's," he said. His father had died suddenly of a heart attack when Mark was 15. He had told me this before. A wave of tender feeling came over me as I realized that Mark had gone off to Salt Lake City to in some way be near to his father.

What had happened after his father died? Did his mother go to work and how was that for him? He had spent a lot of time with his best friend, the one who had visited the previous week. His friend was one year older than Mark and was like a big brother. They had done all their youthful experimenting together. Mark told his friend everything.

Perhaps this is what has happened. Mark's dear friend was here for the weekend and now is gone and Mark never expects to see him again. Perhaps it was like when his father had been there and then was gone, never to be seen again. Mark is very depressed. I think that's why he suddenly gave up.

For the first time in our few weeks of experience, Mark told me he wanted to sleep. Later in the afternoon I saw the psychologist, whom Mark likes very much, and told him some of my concerns. He promised to go by and see him.

I'm having a terrible time with this. I feel like I'm falling apart on the inside. Outwardly, I'm going about my work, but I keep breaking down in tears. Why have I been so affected? How did this happen? This is not a perfect person. Mark is no saint. He's a bit manipulative and controlling. I'm sure he's a pain in the ass at times to friends and family. But I also see the hurts and loves, the scrambling through the pathless brush finding his way. Now here he is at 38; all of it will end too soon. I grieve for him and all the others I may never know.

"God shall wipe away all our tears, and there shall be no more death. Mourning, crying, and pain shall cease, for all former things will pass away." May this comfort promised in Revelations 20 come swiftly, or may some foreshadowing of it cool our sorrow until the day's end.

***

Thursday morning, July 13

A surprising calm has settled over me. It began to come over me yesterday afternoon after writing in this journal. I had been working alone all day. I needed contact with people. I wrote a note to my friend Chris and told him I needed his support. Then I went to my women's health club and worked out with what I've dubbed my "work-out family." Over several years we have gotten to know each other. Several of "the family" are teachers. One, an art teacher, intentionally stayed a few minutes after class to ask me how things were going. I told her what was happening. She said that her daughter's father-in-law and mother-in-law both had died of AIDS. The father was infected several years earlier from a blood transfusion. His wife got the virus from him. Her first-hand experience of AIDS in her family made me feel comfortable with her.

I came home and played Beethoven's Ninth Symphony with enough volume to carry my spirits to a new place. When the part began that is familiar as the hymn "Joyful, Joyful, We Adore Thee," I felt a healing transformation taking place.

Mark, you are pushing me to grow. I'm trying to find the spiritual resources to love and grieve and not be spent, but renewed.

***

42

Thursday evening, July 13

Mark met with his doctor and has stopped all medication. He also is refusing food. Alice, his mother, is back. She and I had a good conversation. We saw Bob, who had stopped by the hospital and spent some good time with Mark.

I went in to see Mark with thoughts about telling him he should eat, that it was selfish to commit passive suicide. But he looked happy and peaceful. Quite spontaneously I leaned over and held him, kissing his face and rocking gently for a few minutes. He was sweetly responsive though weak. There was only a little conversation. With the OK of his nurse, I gave him a foot massage. It was a comfort to him. And it was somehow comforting to me as well. When the foot massage was finished and I sat on the bed next to him, I only wanted to sit there and not to leave. But I was embarrassed to stay longer. Alice had given me this time with him and I knew she was waiting somewhere.

There were seven HIV patients on the unit. I spent some time with each. I felt tender with all of them, even Eddie. Eddie who pushes everyone away. On Tuesday, when I tried to find out a little about him and what support he had, after only a brief time he said, "Too many questions."

Today he was all hooked up to things. A tube was up his nose to carry away fluid from his body. He was miserable. I stood with him awhile with my hand on his. He did not hold mine. His mouth was parched and I gave him sips of water.

I've had cheery days when I was able to be kind and open. When none of it got to me. Today, I was even hugging the nurses. I needed closeness. None of my hugs were turned down. I didn't hug Eddie, but he did say he was disappointed when I told him I had to go. Perhaps sadness has released more of my love and humanity.

Sylvester, a patient I've seen many times, sent me off today with a benediction. How could he know how much I needed it?

Friday morning, July 14

It's not yet 6 in the morning. In the night I kept thinking of Mark, going over things that had been said. And touches. Why have I been so affected? The closeness alone, over so short a time,

43

does not explain it. But my suffering is there and real. In the night I prayed that God would show me a way to let go of Mark. I tried to stay with that prayer.

Finally, about 4:30 this morning, I woke up sobbing, thinking about my sister's death 20 years ago. Because she had committed suicide, I never got to hold her, to comfort her, to see her once more. She was there and then she was gone.

We lived in different towns. When my parents called from their home in Palm Springs to say Martha had committed suicide, I went as quickly as I could. They took me to her apartment. I stood looking at the empty bed where she had died. It had been remade. I never saw her again. She was 38, like Mark.

I had felt so alone, in shock. I remember curling up on our old red love seat in my parents' bedroom. I was alone in the house. My parents had left to make arrangements for burial. Cecil had not yet arrived. I held myself in a fetal position. I felt that all my organs were in disarray, that I was falling apart. And then I was frozen in shock and grief.

I didn't cry much and in a few days I continued my life. No one was there to guide me, to tell me that I had to stay with the grief, keep it fluid until all the anguish had passed. Unknowing, I froze the anguish.

So now here it is 20 years later. In my half sleep I am grieving because I could not hold Martha in my arms and kiss her face and gently rock her, give her comfort. There is one body and one Spirit … One God begetter of us all, who is above all and through all and in all. In the unity of life Mark has let me hold my sister once again and say, "You are loved."

⸻

Sunday, July 16

Late Friday afternoon I went to the hospital hoping to talk with Mark and Alice and tell them what had come to me in the night and to thank Mark.

I had just missed Alice, but Mark was sitting with the bed cranked up all the way. He looked gaunt but was alert. When I came through the door, he said, "I was wanting to talk to you today." A nice welcome. I told him that I also had something I came to tell him. I went first.

I was uncomfortable. This time it was I who was self-revealing. I told him of my crying through the week and praying that a way would be shown me to let him go, and the experience in the night of grieving that I had not been able to hold and comfort my sister at the end of her life. Mark cried when I told him that. It was hard crying for a minute with his whole face involved, not the sad tears slowly welling in his eyes that I had seen before. I had a moment of alarm, perhaps I should not have told him something so upsetting.

After his initial entering into my grief, he asked me questions. When I responded vaguely he pushed me. And he wanted to understand what this all had to do with him. Wasn't it just the circumstances, might it not have happened with any of the patients I have seen?

We were having a real conversation. It had been so easy for me before. I had been like a computer tutor. Whatever Mark inputted was received and I printed out supportive messages. But love and struggle had burst me out of my one-dimensional form. Mark was challenging me and forcing me to be authentic.

When I finished, Mark took his turn. He had had conversations, including a meeting with his doctor. His doctor convinced him that he could not starve himself and die swiftly in a week or so. Mark could go off his medications for awhile, and there was no reason for him to not go home.

In Mark's face I seemed to see a vision of weeks and months of illness, suffering, and fear. He had wanted it to end, and yet, as Robert Frost wrote, "earth's the right place for love: I don't know where it's likely to go better."

Mark told me that Bob and Alice were arranging for a hospital bed. He fumed a little about where they would put it. He would be going home probably the next day. With all the drama that his anticipated death had caused, he looked at me and asked, "Are you disappointed?" "No," I responded, "it will give me a little more time with you to learn how to love with less attachment."

He invited me to stop by his home any time for a cup of tea or coffee. I told him I would like that. As he considered going home, there was a trace of a smile and he said quietly, without looking at me, "More and more the thought pleases me." What thought I asked? "Of not just laying in this bed waiting to die. And of going home," he said.

He proffered suggestions of how I might learn to do this work with AIDS patients, loving with less attachment. He granted that he had no idea how some people, including his good friend Carol, managed it.

I said I needed to go, and he held out his arms and held me to him. It was me receiving comfort this time.

——•+••+•——

45

Monday morning, July 17

Yesterday I attended a memorial celebration for Tom, who had died at the end of June. The celebration was not in a church. It was held at the apartment Robert had shared with Tom. Robert had planned a warm, caring occasion to allow people who had known Tom to come together and share their recollections.

In the AIDS affected community, memorial services in homes and apartments are going on frequently, but this was the first one I had attended.

It was a small, attractive apartment with a little patio by the front door, large windows opening between the living room and patio. People were arriving for about an hour until finally there were around 40 crowded into the living room or outside the open windows on the patio. I was one of the earlier arrivals, warmly greeted and introduced around by Robert as the volunteer who had visited Tom frequently. I was served a glass of champagne and sat in a canvas sling chair watching.

A young gay couple, maybe in their 20s, arrived. One held a bunch of sunny-hued flowers. The young men looked uncomfortable, like boys at a funeral. What are we supposed to do? How should we seem?

A woman arrived with her infant. Robert greeted them and took the baby, cradling it, carrying it around the room, sharing this miracle of new life with guests, then holding it up in the air with love, as though to let everyone see this sign of hope among the milling of the bereaved.

Later, Robert stood in the middle of the room and gathered our attention for a brief time of remembrance. Everyone was being offered a glass of champagne for the toast to Tommy, as they all called him, that would come.

Robert stood in the midst of friends with a glass of champagne in one hand and a greeting card in the other. He told us the message seemed to fit how Tommy would want to be remembered. And then he read it, his hands shaking hard. But he got through it and raised his glass in a toast to Tommy. As I watched what Robert was going through a wave of anger came over me. I was thinking, where is the church that people are having to arrange memorial services in their apartments and homes?

An older man, a playwright, who had known Tommy the longest, had been asked to speak. He told us Tommy had been an ice skater with the Ice Capades. He described seeing Tommy for the first time, when Tommy was about 19 or 20, skating, looking so beautiful. He told us that Tommy had supported himself doing house painting, but that he was an artist and a creative entrepreneur, doing many things. He spoke about the photographs of Tommy on one wall of the living room. I had not noticed them before, about eight 9-by-12 black-and-white professional photographs attractively spanning the width of the room.

Robert had stepped out of the living room and now reappeared with a large painting which he kept turned from us as he explained Tommy's image of the time of death. Tommy had told Robert that when the end was near, if he could not close his own eyes, would Robert close his eyelids. And would Robert remind him that he was heading for the light. Robert then showed us the painting by Tommy which depicted his image of the end. The great arm of God extended across half the canvas and was like the arm and pointing hand in Michelangelo's depiction of Creation. In Tommy's painting the hand was pointing to a sphere of brilliant light. Looking more closely we could see the tiny figure of a man diving into the sphere of light. The small figure was well formed and whole, as Tommy had been one year before.

After the eulogies I walked to the wall and looked at Tommy as the others had known him. I could scarcely imagine he was the same man I had met in the hospital. He had been a gorgeous man, short with a well-developed, athletic body, piercing eyes that were a startling blue, a full, well-defined and sensuous mouth, a cleft chin and prominent facial structure. I stared at the photos in amazement. The man I had known was shrunken. I had seen only the piercing blue eyes and the innate energy of the man. It was like meeting a man when he is very old and having difficulty imagining him as a young man, attracting lovers, starting businesses, making plans, living life.

Late in the afternoon Robert brought out some boxes of pins and earrings Tommy had designed. Robert invited us to take any we wanted. Before I left, I selected a pair of earrings. They were a flat gold, with a burnished gold image of a palm tree on each earring. The shape of the earrings was a small square hanging from one corner, but the edges were slightly uneven. That's what attracted me to them. They weren't exactly what you expected, didn't quite fit the mold, but they were beautiful. They were like Tommy. I'll wear them and remember him.

Wednesday, July 19

Yesterday I felt lonely and at odds when I arrived on the unit. I wanted to see people I already knew. I expect I was experiencing grief.

There were eight HIV patients and most of them were new. It was an effort to start meeting all these new people. I set out down the hall mechanically, room 110 and then room 111. This is the simple method I've developed to be sure to drop in on each patient each time, if possible. In just a few minutes my loneliness was dispelled and I felt engaged. I noticed Eddie was gone and asked Leslie, his nurse, about him. She told me he had gone home. Then she said how bad she had felt because she didn't like Eddie. In four years of nursing, he was only the second patient she had disliked. But she had struggled. She said she had prayed about Eddie. On his last day in the hospital, she had gone in and turned him. He had reached for her hand and took it and said quietly, "Thank you." With the touch and those words all her efforts to relate to him felt worthwhile.

Tender moments. One of the new patients was anxious and on edge but not very revealing in what he was telling me. I kept thinking our conversation was ending, then he would bring up something more. Finally, he told me what was on his mind. His father was right then on the East Coast having brain surgery to remove a malignant tumor. His mother did not know that he also was in the hospital. He did not want to add to her worries, so he was quite alone. Later, I was taking care of an errand for him and came back to his room. He had just called the East Coast and discovered that his father's surgery had gone well. I could see the relief on his face.

Another new patient, Tito, had been nauseated and missed lunch. When he felt better he asked me if I could find a knife to cut a grapefruit someone had brought him. I took it to the kitchen where my friend Ina not only sliced it but divided the sections and garnished each half. I brought them back and he was quite surprised. He's a beautiful dark, lean man, perhaps Chilean, with a charming accent. With an expression of real gratitude, he thanked me and invited me to stop in again "when I was in the area." I thought it was a funny thing for him to say. I told him I would be "in the area" again Thursday afternoon. He said, "Well, that's not too far away." And I felt he really meant it.

Wednesday morning, July 19

I dreamt that Cecil and I were in the car on a street in our neighborhood. It was early evening, still full light as it is now in summer. We were near the elementary school our daughter Ruth attended many years ago. An airplane carrying passengers was coming toward where we were. It was in distress. "I think it's going to come down on the school ground," I said to Cecil. As it got over us, we thought it would make it to nearby Los Angeles International Airport. Then, suddenly, it burst into flames, made a sharp right turn and came down by the school, engulfed in flames.

I awoke disturbed. I felt the dream was about my experience of the AIDS epidemic. All those people on board and they will die. Ruth's school ground was associated with the ages of many of the PLWAs, about the ages of my children. Cecil and I were horrified watchers.

Wednesday afternoon, July 19

I stopped by and saw Mark and his mother Alice. It felt different visiting at Mark's home. He was walking around but was a bit unsteady. I enjoyed seeing them both and seeing Mark in his home. He had described parts of it to me and I was interested to see it. But I felt a little uncomfortable. A visit in his home changed things. We became three-dimensional people. In the hospital we weren't engaged in our usual lives. We were on a set.

Mark sat down on a low stool in the living room to select a record to play. It was the first time I had seen the back of his head. It had always been on a pillow or against a chair. One time I had seen him in the hall, but he was walking toward me. His sandy brown hair is cut in a butch. That much I had seen. But in back it lies down smoothly, soft with a hint of a wave.

He is a man with a home, an architect who takes a great interest in details about his home. And I also have a life outside the hospital. I write funding proposals for non-profits. I go to Santa Monica on Wednesdays to buy organic produce at the Farmers Market, and get computer printer ribbons at an office supply shop nearby.

Mark showed me architectural drawings he had just made for remodeling his house. Mark said it was fun "practicing a little architecture." But he actually would like to start this remodeling! I found it confusing hearing about his plans. To be in life but anticipating death. It's hard to know

49

what direction your feet are headed. He's gaunt. He said that this morning he lost his breakfast.

Later, sitting at the kitchen table with Alice and Mark, he was talking about the evenings he and Bob spend listening to records. I asked Mark how he would characterize his musical tastes. He listed some favorite musicians, names I did not know. "I'm a rock 'n' roller," he said. The words resonated from the deep chest cavity of this tall man and were propelled across the space by that always mobile, small mouth.

A rock 'n' roller. Identity, however juxtaposed with that moment's realities, travels with us to the edge of death.

Rock 'n' rollers should not be dying, not now. I very much want to see my children, to see that they are well and strong. I think it will restore me to see them.

Friday, July 21

Yesterday was an entirely different experience, and pleasant, just an afternoon of visiting. There were six patients on the unit. People who had been feeling quite sick Tuesday were comfortable and talkative today. I went from room to room conversing. By about the third person, I became aware that I was doing something different. We were having real two-way conversations.

When I went to visit Mark last Wednesday in his home, I had realized that I had been wonderful in eliciting patients' stories and feelings but had given them little of myself beyond my care and compassion.

Unconsciously, on this day, I had gotten my whole, ordinary self there. It was more fun, more comfortable. I realized, however, that it is easier to have a normal conversation when the people I am visiting feel more themselves.

As I was gathering my stuff at the nurses' station before leaving, two patients I had introduced to each other came slowly shuffling up. They were in their pajamas and robes and didn't look so great, but they were up. I exclaimed in mock horror, "Oh, my God, they're coming out of their rooms!" This set off a chain of hilarious response with the guys hamming it up and making funny jokes on themselves and one of the nurses stating that this was a self-service hospital. It was a wonderful moment of laughter and community.

Tuesday morning, July 25

Yesterday afternoon I phoned Mark at his home to ask how he was doing. I'd been thinking about dropping by sometime this week, although I didn't say that. By last night, I was looking at my thoughts as I considered dropping by to see him. A prominent feature of my thoughts was wanting to take him something, Haagen Dazs ice cream bars (something I never buy for us), my favorite soy milk, homemade chicken soup. I want him to get better. I want him to gain weight. I want to fix things.

It's so hard to let go of that compulsion. A couple of times when Mark was in the hospital I asked him if there was anything he wanted me to do for him. His answer, "Just be you." The most simple request, yet for me the hardest. It's difficult to believe that value might be attached to the simple act of being me.

In visiting in the hospital, I am trying to stop taking action. Cecil used to be a member of a Zen Buddhist organization. He did Zen meditative sitting at home and also at the zendo, their community building. At the zendo he saw a bumper sticker, "Don't just do something, sit there."

I want to try just sitting there, just being me with these people I'm spending time with. I am glad, if asked, to do errands for the patients. But I want to just be there as fully as possible.

And I want to learn how to be sick, how to be old, how to be who I am when I'm doing little or nothing. I'm learning from the patients. I don't want to be pitiful like Eddie. I don't want to feel I have to control everything done to me like my determined, frantic friend David, the nurse. In whatever state I'm in I want to be "in my own clothes" like Mark. I want to be able to trust others like my friend Ken. I want to be courteous and thoughtful to the end like Neal. I want to be able to laugh and be outrageous like Hugh. I want to take all these people into me as guides for those times, and that time when the active life is not the order of the day. Thanks to all of you teachers.

———————

Wednesday, July 26

Jimmy died this morning. The man with the great round blue eyes, like portholes. The man whose mother was always with him. Just now I phoned the hospital to see how he was and the unit secretary said, "He expired this morning." His mother Ruth has gone. She stayed with him, couldn't be pried from his side, her baby. Then there was only his body. Death came and did what none of us could do, pried him away from her. But we only wanted to take her out for coffee, for a little walk, to talk about the future, to ask what else she might do when Jimmy was gone. But she'd have none of it. She was by his side, massaging his legs, tending to everything, never leaving. Death did it so cruelly. Had she dropped her eyes for a moment? Was there something more she might have done to not lose him?

She told everyone she did not want to live after he was gone. He had been her life. Perhaps I'm wrong. Perhaps death has not pried him away from her. Maybe it's just a walk down the hall. Maybe her life will, in a moment, fly up with him to wherever souls go. Well Jimmy, the musician, it's a wrap.

I'm off balance, not able to work. The epidemic is everywhere because it's in my head all the time. I feel like a survivor in a bombed city, wandering alone through the rubble trying to see something familiar but finding only desolation.

I went to my friend Louise's for lunch. I talked about how I've been feeling. She said, "Have you talked to a therapist recently?" No. We talked about our children. I asked about her husband's business. I stayed three hours.

In the late afternoon I went to my women's health club for my aerobics class. I was comforted to see some of my "work-out family." Nancy calls me Patty, like my mother does. I have felt light-headed all week and wasn't sure I could get through a work-out. But I decided to concentrate on being there with these women, doing something I like. Working out before the mirror, looking in the mirror at all the women of different colors, sizes, shapes, I felt a restoring strength. Women are so wonderful. I must spend more time with women.

—◦⊷•⊷◦—

Sunday 7 a.m., July 30

The last four days I have taken every opportunity to be with friends and to do something different. On Thursday, Cecil and I went to the Getty Museum down on the coast highway. It's a replica of a spacious, airy Roman villa. We spent time looking at the superb Greek and Roman statues and carvings in marble. But my favorite spot was walking through the long, silent herb garden. It runs the length of the villa along its west side. No one else was there. The silence, the symmetry, the beauty of the plants and trees, the order fed me.

Every day since Jimmy's death, I've gone to lunch with friends. Last night Cecil and I met our friends the Bremers for a picnic and outdoor concert at Santa Monica College. The amphitheater was jammed, everyone enjoying the music. I found myself looking over the crowd and wondering, "Does anyone here have AIDS? Wouldn't some of the patients love to be here, if their legs were strong enough to walk up the wide steps, and if they could bring their IVs." The compelling human face of the epidemic has definitely come home to me.

Saturday morning, August 5

My mother is here. We are celebrating her 80th birthday. The family is gathering over a three-day period. Yesterday afternoon, her actual birthday, I left mother and my niece, Kerry, reading and resting and went to see Mark. I felt a little guilty, like I shouldn't be doing something with others on a family day. No one objected. It was just a problem I created in my mind until I explained to myself that Mark is part of my wider family and I wanted to see him.

Last week I had taken him a book I wrote about farm workers and the church. I told him he needn't read the whole book. But I wanted him to read three or four pages at the beginning about me and my point of view. He had read them, and earlier this week we talked on the phone and he said he would like to discuss them with me.

We spent about an hour together yesterday afternoon. He had been to the eye doctor. In addition to having pneumocystis in his eyes, he has a virus called CMV in the left eye. It leads to blindness. It can happen quickly or slowly.

We were sitting in the kitchen at the table. He asked if I would like a glass of wine. We sat sipping white wine while he explained his situation and the treatment options and their likely serious side-effects. He was telling it all calmly. He plans to reject treatment for the eyes. I was looking at those beautiful, still young, light brown eyes. This is an architect, a highly visual person. I wanted to weep.

But he was not crying. He seems to be moving into an acceptance of the losses and the final loss, or is it a gain after his long struggle? I was trying to be in tune with his acceptance. He sees himself moving into the final stage of the illness. Episodes are coming closer together.

It was hot. We moved to chairs in the bedroom, the one room with an air conditioner. He talked about the pages in my book. Had I always been religious? My friend Chris Glaser says spirituality is more intimate than sexuality. This felt like an intimate conversation. We talked about the church and how we each had experienced it. I talked about my own congregation, which publicly welcomes gays and lesbians, and how we had benefited by their presence. He asked how. His direct questions startle me. People seldom ask me direct questions. It's exciting and scary. It forces me to reveal myself. At the point of revelation, I wonder if anything will be there. Are my ideas an illusion?

I have women friends, educated, professional women, who have had my experience of people, especially men, not asking us questions about ourselves or our experience. As an example of this, my daughter Ruth married a fine man from a wealthy, politically conservative family. There was a dinner party the night before the wedding. I was to be seated next to the groom's father and was wondering how we might talk through an entire dinner and avoid a confrontation over our ideas. Then I reassured myself that he would probably never ask me anything about myself but would be happy to talk about himself. I was correct. At the end of the evening, he knew nothing about me.

I gathered my courage to make a response to Mark, who was seated quite upright in his Stickley rocking chair, looking grave. I told him that the congregation has benefited because our gay members are wonderful people. But also, they, along with black members and poor members, carry no illusions about a problem-free life in which one "has it all together." They've had to struggle. Their struggles contribute to our understanding of faith and the meaning of the Gospel.

I talked again about the complex reasons I was doing the hospital volunteer work, the importance to me of the simple treasure of connectedness.

And that was what I was experiencing sitting there with Mark, and what I'm still experiencing a day later. What is the enormous meaning of this connectedness for me? Whatever it is, it fills me. I feel packed with meaning, value, love, and sadness. I'm on a journey and everything is crammed into one bag. Mark is one of my traveling companions who soon will be gone. Gone on his own trip and I will be left behind. All of us will be left behind.

We talked about hair, his hair. I wanted to know how long he had had a butch. About six months. He never liked how fine his hair was and how it just laid down flat. So, he had a butch, and his barber taught him how to make it stand up by rubbing in a little mousse. Mark demonstrated for me, vigorously rubbing his hair, one hand alternating with the other. He said he also had had it frosted, making it that sandy color rather than the darker brown shown in pictures on the table by their bed.

Just before I left, he clambered over the bed to get a picture he especially liked. It was a pic-

Mark and Bob on vacation the summer before I met them.

ture of Mark at 29. Mark and Bob were in front of a vacation cottage. Mark's hair was a little on the long side and a rich brown. The photo caught a sensuous look. It was taken the year he and Bob met.

My heart cries out that youth should last longer, should not be stolen away by the death reach of AIDS. I'm embarrassed to tell him that I'm 54, that we are celebrating my mother's 80th birthday. It feels like having too much money to have had so many years. I want the beautiful young man in the picture to still be here, just a little older. But he won't be.

As I left, he thanked me for having a glass of wine with him.

⊹⊶⊷⊷

Friday 6:45 a.m., August 11

I've had the flu this week. I was alone most of the day Tuesday and feeling sick. In the afternoon I had a low-grade fever. I kept thinking about people with AIDS when they get sick and run fevers in excess of 105 degrees. Thinking of their suffering made me feel worse, but it did put my mild illness into perspective.

I read an article on a gay Buddhist zendo in San Francisco that has been caring for some members with AIDS. Issan Dorsey, leader of the zendo, was interviewed about the hospice. He was asked what he said to one member who wanted to die. Dorsey had said to the young member, "J.D., you'll die when you die. Right now you're alive."

I'm attracted by Buddhist acceptance of things as they are. There are Buddhist activists, but they combine their activism with an acceptance of how things are now.

When I'm sick I lose perspective. I feel helpless and trapped and neurotically feel that it will last forever, even though I know that something like the flu lasts only a few days. Feeling sick with the flu Tuesday, I began to concentrate on accepting the flu in my body. That acceptance gave me a surprising sense of mastery and I could know emotionally that it wouldn't last more than a few days. It was a relief.

I also read a poem by my friend Ivy Dempsey. It's called "Glance."

A moment . . .

I can't see it
but I name it —

My life is passing!

Sometimes I feel
as if, past a window
just behind me — a window
large enough to allow
my whole skeleton
to pass through —

56

my true life waits
for me to enter,
as a wide gleaming river
that flows past everyone —
belongs to everyone —
and is entirely
unnoticed.

Now,
this moment ...
My life is passing!

I got from the poem that every moment is important and a chance to live life fully. Just because we're sick, it doesn't mean life has to be put on hold until we're well. This is probably obvious to many people, but Ivy's poem, my own hospitalizations, and the work with HIV patients have helped me to see this. It gave me a feeling of aliveness and intensity even though I was sick.

By Thursday afternoon I felt well enough to go to the hospital to see the guys on Unit 500. I was weak from not eating much, but I wanted to go. I'm leaving for a two-week vacation in the mountains and wanted to see the patients before I left. There were seven HIV patients on the unit. I didn't feel strong enough to visit all of them, so I decided to visit the ones I knew. Several have been in the hospital other times since I've been volunteering.

Michael was back. He always looked up at me with his big brown eyes like he was there to be taken care of. This time he seemed much more take charge. He told me he had changed doctors. He had remained with his internist for the more than two years since his diagnosis. Now he is being seen by two doctors specializing in HIV, and they have access to experimental drugs.

Michael described an earlier experience with the doctor trying to find a vein to start his IV. He stuck Michael 10 times and never succeeded in finding a vein. Before the tenth time the doctor said, "One more time." And Michael had said, "That's right, one more time and that's it."

His new doctor has surgically implanted a Hickman catheter so Michael won't be stuck anymore. He expressed relief about that.

The assertive Michael seemed quite different to me than the sweet Michael with the trusting eyes of a 5 year old. I was aware that I was with a man. I was glad he was acting on his own behalf.

Roy was back. After his last hospitalization he had had four good days before things began to fall apart: anemia with accompanying weakness and a violent reaction to too large and direct a dose of chemotherapy, a treatment for Kaposi's sarcoma. Roy is a reserved man. This is the fourth time he's been in. We've slowly gotten to know each other. This time he was much more directly expressive of his feelings. He was angry and aggravated about how the chemo was given to him at another hospital, the long and needless wait at the doctor's office, and the sloppy admitting process when he came to the hospital this time,

He said, "I've done a good job of learning to live with AIDS. I've accepted that I'm going to die. It's all this other bullshit that really gets to me."

I had a couple of other visits and then knew I had to quit. I felt light-headed and needed to go back to bed myself. I didn't want to leave and didn't want to say goodbye to the guys on unit 500. Two weeks can be eventful in the life of a PLWA. A lot can happen and a lot can end.

From home I called Bryle, the nursing supervisor, and asked him to leave a message on my home phone if Mark was readmitted while I was away. I will be calling in for messages and want to know if he's in the hospital. God only knows why I want to know, especially while I'm on vacation. But I guess I want my inner thoughts about Mark to more closely match what is actually happening. At best it will only be a rough approximation.

While I'm in the mountains I want, somehow, to continue on an inner level relating to the men I've met who have AIDS. These relationships and what I am learning from them are the most important thing happening in my life. I have no desire to take a vacation from that. But I look forward to leaving the crowded city with its thousands of cars and its always accelerated pace. I just came across this poem attributed to naturalist John Muir:

> *Climb the mountains,*
> *and get their good tidings.*
> *Nature's peace will flow into you*
> *as sunshine flows into trees.*
> *The winds will blow their own freshness into you,*
> *and the storms their energy,*
> *while cares will drop off*
> *like autumn leaves.*

Tuesday morning, August 15
Woods Lodge, Mammoth Lakes

Dear Mark,

We're staying in a cabin about 500 feet above the lake in the picture. We've stayed at this lake many times and in this particular cabin for the last six years. The resort is called Woods Lodge. We're a few miles out of Mammoth.

It's high — 9,500 feet elevation. It takes a few days for our bodies to adjust. Last summer we came up five weeks after I had a hysterectomy. I was anemic before the surgery and more so after. When I got up to this high altitude, all I felt like doing for a couple of days was resting and reading. The few valiant red cells in my body were rushing around trying to do the work of many. The good news was that the altitude shoved my body into accelerated production of red cells, which was helpful when I returned to sea level.

You would love the quiet here. Inside the cabin it is completely still. Outside the cabin, in the Lodge pole and white pine forest, there is what I call a lively silence, a silence made more sweet and healing by bird songs and the slight and constant movements caused by the gentle wind. By the lakes and streams there is water noise, water lapping, water moving. The sound of water is my favorite sound.

Several years ago Cecil and I went to Yosemite in early spring for cross-country skiing. We drove up from Los Angeles and arrived just before dusk. We unpacked the car and took a walk toward the falls. We were alone on the path in the gathering dark. We crossed the larger bridge, walking into the woods. We came upon a second, smaller bridge that crossed a shallow stream, where the water flowed with energy over rocks.

I stopped, wept to hear the sound, so welcomed, like the voice of an old friend I had not heard in a long time.

There are some spots of lively silence in Los Angeles. If you feel up to it when I return, we could visit one or two.

We generally spend two weeks when we come to Lake George. I spend a lot of time reading. We hike, eat, and make love. It's a time for getting my scattered self back together. You haven't known my typically scattered self, trying to do more than time allows, choosing with frustration between this and that. In the time we've spent together, I've been all there and glad for it.

Lake George is one of a series of lakes. When we hike to Mammoth Crest we get views of the

59

lakes — Crystal emptying into George, George emptying into Lake Mary, Mary into Mamie and on along the chain.

I think people are like this. That which is good, which is God in us, flows from one to another, keeping each in turn refreshed.

There are aspects of you which have refreshed me.

The availability of your thoughts and feelings have flowed into me and filled me up.

Your love of your family, of Lisa, Joshua, your niece Katie have refreshed me. Your respect and appreciation for your mother are beautiful, as is your valuing of your father, wearing his ring, attending his college. I've enjoyed your variety of expressions of love for Bob.

Our love for others is never pristine. It's always mixed with anger, and wishing certain things were a bit different, and trying to get what we want in ways that may not work well. But the love itself endures and is good.

I've also been refreshed by your uniquely creative ways of thinking and expressing yourself. You have a wonderfully creative, concrete turn of mind. It must be the gifts of the architect in you — creative and concrete. One afternoon when we were visiting at the hospital, you were telling me about being sick that morning. You talked about having a "diarrhea party." Who else would ever put those two words together? It will always improve my thoughts about diarrhea.

I hope you stay out of the hospital while I'm gone. I can't say why exactly, but I know it would distress me for you to be in the hospital while I'm vacationing.

I hope you can read my handwriting without too much difficulty. I saw your writing in your address book and it was beautiful. A typewritten letter would have been easier than my handwriting. But, alas, hauling my IBM Selectric up here would seem excessive.

Write me here if you care to, or send a picture you draw. Otherwise, I'll expect to speak with you when I return.

With affection,
Pat Hoffman

❖

Thursday, August 17
Woods Lodge

Cecil read the more recent pages of my journal, and we talked about some of the issues the hospital work raised for me. I told him more about the conversation Mark and I had had about religion and the church.

I would not have had that conversation with Mark if he had not brought it up. I feel that people, at least "straight" people like myself, in the institutional church have to earn the right to speak of faith to gay men. Much of the church has been so rejecting of gay men that we have lost the right, the opportunity to speak about spiritual issues. First we have to demonstrate love, not for who they might become, but love for who they are, even a rejoicing in the gay men God created them to be. Gay men with AIDS provide us in the church an occasion for serving in simple, unassuming ways. This may be all that "straight" people in the church can do right now in the AIDS epidemic.

Talking about this with Cecil, I burst into tears, I felt it so vehemently — at 9 in the morning yet.

What is this hot magma that lies beneath my surface and can suddenly rise and erupt? What is the source of this identification?

Between the ages of 1 and 6 I was a little nomad, traveling from place to place with my musician father, my mother, and older sister. I could form no attachment to place or people, other than my family and two or three musicians who traveled with us — a fat, alcoholic organ player named Bob, and Chuck, a thin man who played bass.

My sister and I were always outsiders. We developed a fierce identification with anyone considered outsiders by "the stable ones." This was in spite of the fact that my memories, from after our settling in Los Angeles when I was 9, are of feeling accepted by schoolmates, neighborhood children, and friends from church. My sister Martha's experience seemed similar. Once we settled down she had friends and seemed popular.

This early experience of being an outsider may be the source of my identification with "those beyond the pale," the pale being a stake in a fence demarcating a boundary. I spent formative years as one always coming from beyond the pale, yet I felt myself to be a good and valuable person, or wanted to believe I was.

Gay men, when they are known to be gay men, are generally considered beyond the pale by the institutional church and much of society.

Some of the anger and tears must be in my own defense. See me, this little blond child, I am worthy of inclusion. Had anyone doubted it? Maybe only me, and perhaps I still do.

———•◦•———

Thursday evening

I called home for messages this afternoon. The last message was from Byrle. Mark is back in the hospital. There were other messages as well and things to be taken care of.

It was a pay phone outside the lodge and I felt the evening chill at this High Sierra lake. I was shaking with cold, but more from distress. I returned a call from a minister friend, Art French, who wanted to be sure Cecil and I had heard that another friend, Tom Phelps, had died. Yes, we had. He died on Aug. 4, his 65th birthday and my mother's 80th.

I told Art that I had just learned that a friend with AIDS was back in the hospital. He heard my distress and understood how I must feel 300 miles away.

I hung up and hastily, nervously put my Foncard in the wallet slot and stacked wallet, address book, and note pad to leave. But I couldn't. With shaking fingers I pulled out my Foncard again, looked up the number for the hospital, and started entering all the required numbers. I reached the hospital tape and entered the extension number for Unit 500.

Mary, one of the unit secretaries, answered. I asked her how Mark was. She said he was not good mentally. I was alarmed, thinking it was neurological damage, and was actually reassured when she explained that he was upset and anxious. I asked if I could speak with him. Mary said he had just returned from having a CAT scan and was pretty upset about a long delay. She didn't know if he would want to talk on the phone. I asked her to check. In a minute Mark came on the phone.

He has a deep, resonant voice that matches his over 6-foot frame. It was good to hear his voice. And it made me feel good that he wanted to speak with me. He reported what had been happening. He had once again become dehydrated and was not able to get enough nourishment. He had become extremely weak and had been falling down at home.

I felt some confusion about when different things had happened. I asked when he had been admitted and he said Monday. I was surprised that Byrle had not called my home until Wednesday. I told Mark I had written him a letter. He said he had received it on Monday or Tuesday. I had not mailed it until Tuesday. Being sick and in the hospital can be pretty disorienting, various medicines

62

for sleep or pain can cause this, as well. Mark reported that he has fever and is in a lot of pain.

He mentioned the picture postcard I had enclosed with my letter, a card showing Lake George. "It's beautiful. It must be a very special place for you and Cecil … And your letter was beautiful." His words hung there laden with meaning and feeling, all unexplained. I could only guess.

I've been reading Madeleine L'Engle's journal "A Circle of Quiet." She wrote at one point, "Grandma gave me herself, and so helped to give me myself." That's what I wanted to do in my letter to Mark, to give him something of myself to help him know the gift of something of himself.

I told Mark I wished I was there. He said he wished I was too, that, "it would help." That he wants me there makes it more painful. I told him I would have him in my thoughts and would phone again. He said, asking a question, "I'll see you in a week?" Yes, about a week.

Will I see Mark again? He could die before I return. May the Spirit of God be present with him and hold him in loving arms.

◦─◦◦■◦◦─◦

Friday morning, 8:45 a.m., August 18
Woods Lodge

Dear Mark,

I had a terrible sleep last night thinking of you sick and in pain. I didn't want to dwell on those thoughts because it seemed useless and impotent. But most of the time we have little control over our feelings. So, I am trying to receive, accept my fretting and distress, and hope that in some small, unimaginable way, it may serve the cause of goodness, which I call God.

In the spring, shortly before I began visiting at the hospital, I read "An Interrupted Life," the 1941–43 diaries of Etty Hillesum, a young Dutch Jew. She recorded the ever-tightening circle around Jews in Amsterdam and the fear and worry. She was in her 20s and searching for inner resources to meet the Holocaust that was occurring and her own anticipated end.

I was terribly impressed with her capacity for joy and gratitude for beauty. I'm trying to learn from that young woman. This morning, looking across the forest to this beautiful lake, I'm trying to be open to feelings of gratitude for beauty and for love and for the gifts of knowing people and of knowing you, Mark.

All of these gifts are held gently in my hands along with my sorrow for your suffering.

My friend Chris Glaser intends to stop by the hospital tomorrow, Saturday, to bring you something from me. I told him you said you do not feel like having strangers come to visit, so I'm sure he will be in tune with your wishes.

May that goodness which I call God surround you and hold you in this difficult time.

As ever,
Pat Hoffman

Saturday morning, August 19
Woods Lodge

All day Friday I felt upset about Mark being in the hospital. Late in the day I took a walk alone, hoping to sort out my feelings. The question which bubbled to the surface was, "Am I doing all I can?" Am I doing all I can? Of course not! But how much is required? How much is appropriate? I reminded myself that I'm an AIDS Project Los Angeles (APLA) volunteer. My commitment was to see patients in the hospital and provide liaison with APLA for those who are APLA clients. I had, with full knowledge, transgressed one of the APLA guidelines when I kept in contact with Mark after he left the hospital. I'm sure those guidelines are designed to give us limits and to help protect against burn-out. With the guidelines I could answer the questions of how much is required and appropriate.

Mark and I have become friends of a special kind and now I was on my own with these troubling questions. We still have, in a way, a "hospital friendship." But we have each given more than is typical. And we each have, for our own reasons, involved the other. We have become important to each other.

The question, "Am I doing all I can?" led to thoughts about showing love. I feel that I love Mark, but I would be challenged to say what that means. I think it has something to do with care about the other person and with an acceptance of the other person. Mark has been plainspoken about practices and experiences that I would not myself engage in (having nothing to do with homosexuality, I might add). And he has at times spoken harshly and judgmentally about others, including other patients, though Byrle told me that might be a result of the disease process. Regardless of the cause, I accept this about him. I accept these things about him because I have not lived in his skin and am not now experiencing the stress and anxiety of serious illness and all that goes with it. I see around these things to a man of love, loyalty, tenderness. A man trying to live his life. Perhaps this is love. If I do love Mark, what are the requirements of love?

I finished my walk part way around the lake and back up the hill toward the cabin without resolving these questions. I felt nervous and unsettled.

At 5 p.m. I phoned the hospital again. I spoke to Pat, the other unit secretary. She told me Mark was very depressed. I asked to speak with him. Alice answered the phone and put Mark on.

He wanted to talk with me, but it wasn't much of a conversation. He sounded zonked on medication. He was confused and formed his thoughts and words slowly. He asked if we had spoken that morning or the day before and wondered if he had called me or I had called him on that previous occasion.

I wanted a real conversation with Mark. I wanted to know how sick he is, how near the end he may be. But he could scarcely answer my questions. Yes, he had slept well the night before. Yes, he still had pain. Yes, he was on a lot of medication for pain and sleep, and with effort he named some of them. Then something happened, perhaps the nurse arrived or something, and he indicated that he needed to leave the line. It was unclear and I didn't understand. But Mark said to me, "I love you." And I responded, "I love you, Mark." Then he seemed to leave the line and I hung up.

His words brought me instant rest. I felt somehow a resolution to my anxious worrying about whether I had done all I could. His expression of love put me at rest. There were no conditions. The love was for me, just as I am. What a precious gift.

—◦—◦—

Sunday, 4:15 p.m., August 20
Woods Lodge

It's raining out. An hour ago there was hail. Low clouds hang over the mountain peaks and there is thunder.

I need to grieve, to cry, to let the tears come down like the rain, to feel the chill of the hail. I'm thinking about Mark and about those who have died, Neal, David, Tommy, Jimmy. But I'm on vacation with my husband. Our close friends the Bremers are here for the weekend. If I cried, were congruent with my feelings, I would spoil it for them. If I caught the Greyhound back to Los

Angeles to be present with Mark, Cecil would feel lonely and abandoned.

Cecil knows I'm thinking of Mark. About once a day he asks me, "How are you?" Yesterday he bought a Hershey's candy bar and left half as a surprise for me. He was disappointed when I didn't notice it and set it in the nosepiece of my glasses. When I found it, I thought how sweet that was, but forgot to say so. Later, he asked me if I found his gift for me.

I'm afraid I'm not there for Cecil or Mark or myself.

———•⊷•———

5 p.m.

I called home for messages on my answering machine. I had to listen to all the messages from earlier in the week because my remote has not been erasing them. I listened through eight previous messages, then there were two new ones. Alice called at 11 a.m. today and left the home number, Mark and Bob's home, where she is staying. She said she very much wants to speak with me. The other message came later in the day and was from Chris Glaser. I had asked him to visit Mark for me, to take him a yellow flower and give Mark a hug for me. Chris thought he would go on Saturday, then changed to Sunday afternoon. The message Chris left for me was that Mark is in a coma. Chris said he spent an hour talking with Alice.

I must decide what I will do. Mark told me about being in a coma last year for six days. Everyone was so worried, but he was "on the other side of the moon." I guess he's on the other side of the moon again, but I'm here on earth and am in sorrow. I feel the need to see him before he is gone.

———•⊷•———

9 p.m.

I've been trying to reach Alice. I called the hospital again and spoke with Mark's nurse. Mark slipped into a deep coma Saturday. The doctor thinks he may die within 24 hours.

Mark's nurse said Alice was not there but "the significant other" was. I asked to speak with Bob. He is reserved and private about his feelings. I told him I was considering coming down for a day or two but wanted to know how he would feel about that. He was frank in letting me know that I could visit if I wanted, but he would not want me to stay. He explained the schedule. He is there in the morning and evening. Alice is there in the afternoons and is staying at night. I told him I would call Alice at home.

Alice and I had a good conversation. She said she has felt at peace since Mark slipped into the coma. He had been agitated before and anxious that he might be experiencing dementia, though his confusion and difficulty forming words could be related to medication. I told her my thoughts about coming back to Los Angeles for a day or two. She brought a lot of realism to bear on that decision. First, she described Mark's condition, his noisy breathing, the nurse coming in frequently to suction saliva from his mouth. She suggested that I remember him as I had known him. Besides, there could be no guarantee that he would be living when I arrived. She said they are planning a memorial service and would let me know about it.

I cried when I talked with Bob and I cried when I talked with Alice. I was the only one crying. Well, that's me and that's to be accepted, too.

We all have to live out our own experience. Perhaps my grief is heightened because I'm far away and can't touch him or see him or directly enter into the experience. I want to be there, but extraordinary steps to get there don't seem appropriate for me, the volunteer visitor.

I will not make a special trip to Los Angeles. I will cherish our final words, "I love you." "I love you, Mark." Isn't this the one great gift we can give and can receive? Beyond that is just motion.

◦•❖•◦

Monday, August 21

This afternoon I placed a long-distance call to the hospital and spoke with Val, the charge nurse. "Is Mark still living?" "No, he died early this morning."

It's over. We gave each other some comfort and support for a few miles, his last miles.

After I got the news, Cecil and I went walking through the woods to the lower lakes. When we got to the road that goes around Lake Mary and started across the bridge, there were three young men fishing from the bridge. Out of my unconscious, uncontrolled mind sprang a feeling of resentment that they were there, alive, while Mark was dead. I was chagrined with my uncharitable thoughts and reminded myself that these were some mothers' sons, good and valuable people.

The walk was quiet, on paths around the lakes, down to Lake Mamie and around to the Lake Mamie store. I looked around with no desire to purchase anything, just passing some time.

Walking back through the woods, I was thinking how I have never had much courage for physical adventures. But I have had interpersonal adventures. When I chose to become close to Mark, I did so knowing he would soon die, knowing the loss would be painful. And it is. But I would not have done otherwise. I don't know if this is courage, but maybe it is.

I did all I could to be faithful to my own sense of call. This man came into my life and found that I had something to offer him in his distress. I listened to his anxiety. I brought a little companionship during long afternoons. I received his anger and anxiety with no inclination to judge or recommend. A miracle for me. I watched his tears and heard some sad goodbyes.

But in the end my gifts to him became indistinguishable from his gifts to me. He gave me gifts of trust and affirmation. He entered into my resurrected grief for my sister with tenderness and compassion. He let me hold him and held me. When we let ourselves know it, we are all at the edge of the great aloneness, longing for moments of closeness.

In the ancient Christian tradition we pass the peace as we touch one another, touch hands, embrace, or give the kiss of peace. The traditional words we share are, "The peace of God be with you … And also with you."

Perhaps we do not so much give one another love as touch one another and pass God's love to each other. Mark's last words will stay with me a long time and strengthen me. They are God's love passed on to me.

⚬—•—⚬

Tuesday morning, August 22
Woods Lodge

Dear Bob and Alice,

I will not be at the memorial service Friday evening. Cecil and I will not be returning home until Sunday. I was grateful for the message about the memorial, Alice.

This has been painful for me. More painful than one would expect under what seems to be the circumstances as far as I am concerned.

I've been visiting at the hospital on behalf of APLA for three months. Alice, you and Mark and Mark's dog Arlo were among the first people (and the only dog) I met. I met you the first day I was there. All four of the patients who were there that first day have died, plus one other man. I felt involved with each of them at some level.

But Mark was unique, and the bond that developed between us was both surprising and unique. I want to tell you something about that from my perspective.

In those first days, Mark seemed to me to be experiencing a great deal of anxiety which got expressed in talking, sometimes nonstop. I'm sure you remember this. In my two afternoons a week at the hospital, I would spend perhaps 30 minutes attentively listening to whatever Mark wanted to talk about. I remember hearing a lot about Lisa and Joshua and Katie, Lisa's children, about the purchase of Arlo and expressions of his fondness for that dog. He also talked about some of his early experiences related to AIDS. Alice, you were present for some of that, and for some of Mark's comments about how surprised he was, Bob, that you stayed with him after he was diagnosed — how important that was to him.

I think the time I spent listening was a little help in providing surcease of his anxiety. And for myself, I felt affirmed that he wanted to spend time talking to me.

By the next time Mark was in the hospital, things had changed. What I noticed most was despair and sorrow. I do not remember quite the flow of things at that point. But I remember the discouragement and the tears. Sitting with him, watching the tears and hearing his thoughts drew me in. Never the dispassionate observer, I became involved in his experience. I cared about what was happening and felt like a privileged listener.

In a subsequent hospitalization, the staff would sometimes ask me to be sure to go in to see Mark, that he was depressed or angry or whatever. They never needed to ask me because I always wanted to see him. I'm new in this role of hospital visitor and I won't deny that the staff's confidence in me and Mark's affirmations fed me and reassured me.

The decisive turn in our developing relationship came on the Monday after Bob Hansen and his family left. Mark and I spoke on the phone and he asked me to come to the hospital, that he had something important to speak with me about. I went with a little reluctance. Should I take time away from work for a special trip to the hospital, not on one of my regular days? But basically, I wanted to respond and did. When I got there, he told me he wanted to "let go" and had asked for agreement from you, Bob, and from Alice, Carol, and Lisa. Now he was asking if it was OK with me.

I was dumbfounded by his request and not able to respond as requested. We had an intense conversation, with me asking him questions, trying to understand what was going on with him. He had seemed so cheerful a few days before, looking forward to his friend's arrival.

Some of the pieces began to come together, at least in my mind. But at that point, an entirely new dynamic took over, unexpected and unwelcomed.

Mark had invited me into his life at a deep and emotional level. I, never wary of such involvement, in fact drawn to it, had accepted the invitation and probably encouraged it. He was saying to me, "Is it OK with you for me to let go?" I was responding, "No, it's not OK with me. I need more time with you."

I was in grief that entire week, barely functional, praying for relief, praying for understanding of my inordinately strong response. On Thursday of that week, in the night, I awakened sobbing and thinking of my sister, my only sibling, who took her own life at the age of 38. This had happened 20 years before. But on that Thursday night, for the first time, I was able to be consciously aware of the grief I had carried all these years because I had been unable to hold her, comfort her, see her at the end. She was there and then she was gone.

Mark's gift to me was that he let me be close to him, to hold him and give a little comfort. In a strange way that reaches beyond conscious understanding, he gave me the opportunity I had missed so long ago.

That Friday afternoon I went to the hospital to share this with Mark. He, in turn, told me of his decision to resume eating and go home for awhile. He invited me to visit him at home, which, as you know, I did on three occasions. Our "hospital friendship" had been changed. We were both more fleshed out. Seeing Mark at home was an entirely different experience for me than seeing him in the hospital. I got a much stronger sense of him as an architect, as a man with all the day-to-day elements that make up our lives.

And there was a new, and at times uncomfortable, demand on me to be more real and who I am. Mark had a marvelous directness about him. It would startle and challenge me.

I cannot say that I have learned what I would like to have learned about letting go of another person. But I think I have learned something about it in this process. And I have learned some things about myself. And I have definitely learned — even with all the tears — that risking loving and being loved is worth it.

I write you this long letter because I may not see either of you again. I have felt some need for review and some need for closure. I don't think a person ever has enough experience to know how to do these things. I'm trying.

I wish for you comfort in the loss of this beautiful, deep, funny, expressive, wonderful man.

With affection,
Pat Hoffman

After writing to Bob and Alice I spent the day in prayer and reflection. In the afternoon Cecil and I took a beautiful hike along a stream to Sky Meadow. On the way, I was memorizing a prayer by Dag Hammarskjold, who served as Secretary General of the United Nations. The prayer appears in the Oxford Book of Prayers. The prayer kept my mind fixed on God who has the power to heal.

Yesterday I found myself thinking compulsively about Mark, or myself, going over interactions, reviewing what I had written in two letters to him (the second of which was received after he was comatose). This compulsive reviewing made me miserable and quite unavailable to Cecil.

Today, memorizing Hammarskjold's prayer displaced the compulsive thinking and refocused my thoughts. Certain lines were especially helpful:

And may I never despair for I am under thy hand.
Keep me in thy love as you wouldest that all be kept in mine.

—◦•╫•◦—

Wednesday, August 23
Woods Lodge

At points of stress, my old personal and relational problems come forward. Cecil and I have had tension off and on since we got here, each feeling we are not accepted by the other in the way we want. My old issues of wanting to be loved unconditionally and wanting help and encouragement with my life and work have come up.

I haven't prayed much today.

—◦•╫•◦—

This morning I am thinking with pain that this evening at 6 p.m. will be the memorial service for Mark. I'm in pain because I will not be there for the time of remembrance and closure. But perhaps at a deeper level I am in pain because the service appears to be the final tie with this person I allowed myself to love and be loved by. I don't want to acknowledge that that opportunity for closeness and mutuality has ended.

———•×•×•———

3:40 p.m.

I haven't felt well today. Am I somatizing my sadness?

———•×•×•———

Evening

We had dinner at the cabin as usual. But I wanted distraction. We drove to the Mammoth Crest Viewpoint and watched the sun set behind a range aptly called the Minarets. We walked around a little. It was cold.

When we started back through Mammoth, I told Cecil I didn't want to go back to the cabin yet. How about going out for pie and coffee? We went to The Stove, a cozy family restaurant. Seated at our booth, I was watching families eating dinner. A young father, ready to leave, was standing in the aisle holding his baby, gently kissing the baby's face. I imagined Mark's father 38 years ago, holding Mark, kissing his little face. He and Alice could not have known all that would happen, how he would be snatched away at age 38. This young father with his baby is filled with the moment. And that's as it should be.

Sunday we leave the Mammoth Lakes and return to Los Angeles.

———•×•×•———

Tuesday, August 29

Late August and we're back in Los Angeles. I went to the hospital this afternoon. I wanted to find out details about Mark's last days. One of the nurses gave me a welcome back hug and told me Mark died the day before she returned from her honeymoon. She said she missed him. His nurse at the end was not on duty today. But Mitch was on and had been Mark's nurse before he became comatose. He told me a few details.

There were seven HIV patients on the unit. I visited all of them. David, the nurse, was back. He has pneumonia, but was fairly well and energetic today. He told me he brought along a bear I had given him. He said he likes it and is going to pass it on to someone else when he no longer needs it.

I ran into Ina from the dietician's office. We hugged and spoke of Mark's death. One of the longtime volunteers came along the hall and spoke with me. She reads the obituaries every day and said we had lost a patient. I thought she meant Mark, but she noted that he was 62. Well, that wasn't Mark. Then I said, "Did Ken die?" Yes, that was the name. Ken had died on Aug. 22. I wasn't expecting that. Dear man. Now he won't have to solve the difficult problem of finding someone to live with him. He had been worrying about that. I will miss him.

I saw the staff psychologist in the hallway as I was leaving the hospital. He told me he had gone to the memorial for Mark. I wanted to ask everything about it, but he seemed to be on his way someplace, so I didn't. I don't even know where the memorial was held. I'd like to picture it. I want to talk about Mark with people who knew him and there aren't many of those in my life. I need help.

Wednesday, August 30

This was the first day I've had alone since before vacation. It felt important to be alone. I felt sad. There has been nothing I really wanted to do. I took care of some washing and ironed a lot of clothes. I went to the Farmers' Market in Santa Monica and it made me think of Mark. The first time I went to see him and Alice at his home was on my Farmers' Market day. I'm experiencing many associations with Mark. Most are details he shared about himself. In three months, all these associations have built up.

Teresa and Hank Bremer visited us while we were at Woods Lodge. Teresa wanted to know all about the hospital visitation work. She and Hank were with us when I found out that Mark was back in the hospital and when I got the news of his death. She understood my sorrow and my sense of isolation. Teresa is a psychotherapist and three of her clients had died. She cared about them. She knew so much about them, details of their lives. Then they were gone, and she had no place in the circle of grieving. No one I know knew Mark, except the nurses at the hospital. There is a feeling of painful isolation, and wanting some kind of contact with the person who has died.

This afternoon when the mail came, there was a brief, warm letter from Alice. Enclosed was a printed piece from the memorial with a picture of Mark. It was a head shot and I believe I recognize the picture. I think it was cropped from a photo Mark had with him at the hospital. It was a picture of him and Bob taken last summer on their vacation. It was in that picture that I had noticed his hair style had been changed. Before it had been darker and cut differently. It's a lovely picture and I so appreciate having it.

Alice's letter was full of grace and balm. Reading it released my tears, which had only leaked out from time to time over these days. I just cried and cried. I had so needed some contact with someone important in Mark's life.

She said in her letter that she hoped I would have the strength to continue visitation at the hospital. I hope I have the strength, too. Her encouragement will definitely help.

Thursday, August 31

Hugh also died last week. I talked to Byrle today. He had a phone call from Hugh's family back East. Hugh died peacefully at home. That was what he wanted.

He handled his illness so well. A brilliant, gifted, outrageous, warm man. Did you have long enough to leave the mark you wanted to leave, Hugh?

Monday, September 11

It's fall. I have been dragging through the last two weeks. A good day, a couple of bad days, depression and fatigue, then a lifting of my spirits. I'm trying. I've been so focused on the work at the hospital that I have ignored some other big dynamics in my life this spring and summer. Their reality came crashing through during the last two weeks.

Last Wednesday I had abdominal pains. I thought it was something I had eaten and kept working. Thursday afternoon it was hard to walk without crumpling over, so I didn't visit at the hospital. Friday evening I had a fever. I guess it was the flu again, the third time in two months. I spent Saturday in bed with an Anne Tyler novel. I didn't want the book to end. I didn't want the day to end. By the end of the day Saturday I was better, unfortunately. That meant I must resume responsibilities, which I did on Sunday morning, but without spirit.

In the late afternoon Sunday, Cecil and I went walking in Temescal Canyon. We listened to the crickets and heard the quiet. A thought of Mark and his longing for quiet brought a rush of sadness.

First thing this morning I was clearing up ironing as I usually do early in the day and singing "Create In Me a Clean Heart, O God," which I also characteristically do while I iron. I sing our congregation's liturgical music while I'm starting the day. But it didn't fill my whole mind.

This question came: What is the meaning of developing a loving, encouraging relationship with someone who is about to die? With that question I knew I was like the doctors who are criticized for thinking only of prolonging life.

I'm a mother three times over. I've been a mother for 33 years. I've had some exciting jobs, but parenting has been my biggest, longest-lasting job. What I've learned in it, how I've done it, has put an enormous imprint on me. I've done my very best to love my children, to accept and welcome them as the individuals they are. And it has always been my hope that my love and acceptance would free them to fulfill their hopes and possibilities. It was always love for the future, love for the fulfillment of life.

I've practiced on my children and tried to live that out with others. Now I'm confronted with what it means to love and encourage someone who is about to die, who is not moving into hopes and possibilities as we have known them. Is the value of such relationships mainly for me, so that I might feel good about myself: what a fine, loving, accepting person I am? Is it enough to perhaps provide a few moments of comfort in the closing weeks of someone's life? And sometimes I can't even do that, sometimes I can't mesh the ways I show love with the other person's style, what they like. The last three times at the hospital, I felt inept. I missed, much of the time, with the patients I saw.

Glenn, an older man, very sick, very anxious, told me he wished I wouldn't touch him, that it really bothered him. Another guy is from New York. He got sick while visiting in Los Angeles. When he told me about it, I didn't gush. I think I said, "Oh," with a little downward drop at the end. He shot back that it wasn't an "Oh" thing, he was doing fine and would be going home soon.

Maybe it's me. Maybe I'm needing too much myself right now and patients are picking it up.

But the fact is that sometimes I can't even provide a little support or comfort. So, what's the point of being there? I wonder if doctors sometimes feel this way, or nurses?

I'm so full of questions. I want answers. I want a clear road. I want a definite sense of direction. This is the third time I've used the word definite in this journal in the last two or three weeks. That says something. I want things to be definite. How can life be definite when it is suspended on an undulating sea of questions?

———◦•◦———

Sunday, September 17

This week I've been sick again. I was OK Sunday, Monday, Tuesday, then was back in bed. I work like the dickens and get exhausted and then am sick again.

I'm too intense. Yesterday, in early evening, Cecil and I walked out on the long jetty at Marina del Rey. We watched sailboats coming into harbor. There was scarcely any wind and most of the boats were motoring in. One sailboat, a Coronado 25, was coming in very slowly. The motor was silent. A couple sat visiting on the deck. They seemed unconcerned about speed. Their sails were still unfurled, but with no wind, they were lax, lufting.

I go through life heading into the wind, my sails taut.

There's a time to relax and let them luft.

———◦•◦———

Tuesday, September 19

Today I returned to the hospital. The patients have been moved to another wing while rooms in Unit 500 are refurbished. There were four HIV patients. I had met all of them before.

One was sitting in a chair watching TV, wearing a baseball cap. He makes a show of cheerfulness. He doesn't know who this woman is who enters his room and asks how he is doing. I spend a minute or two and our conversation stays on the surface.

Another man, another Ken, was sitting up in bed working on a project on this overbed table. He put it aside when I came in. I stood at the end of the bed. He told me of his relief that they have identified what was making him sick and they are now treating it. He was feeling quite well. I was struck by the beauty of his calm gray eyes. He looked directly at me as he spoke. He works in a scientific field and relates with ease to medical information as it is available to him. I made that observation to him. He acknowledged it and then said, "It was scary when they didn't know what was making me sick."

Another patient, Howard, looked so much better today. A week ago he was shivering under a pile of blankets, very sick, very vulnerable. He had always greeted me with a facade. I had been careful not to trespass when he was vulnerable.

Today he surprised me. He talked about his facade, that it is gone, that there is a new persona and he doesn't quite know the new person yet. I asked about his work. He used to be a ballet dancer and also has been a dancer/actor. He writes as well. He talked about what is always important, whatever the circumstances: compassion and creativity. He hopes to write about what is happening to him. As we talked, I noticed his exceptional hands, large with extraordinarily long brown fingers. Before I left, I mentioned how beautiful his hands were and touched one lightly before I left.

I hope to see him again before he is discharged. I want to thank him for his trust.

Friday, September 22

I feel a shift in my way of relating to these men. It's been developing. Now I feel it is taking hold, becoming natural for me. The mothering role has been left behind somewhere. With that gone, something different has happened to my experience of the expression in my eyes. I picture myself before with an empathetic look of sadness in my eyes. I call them my cocker spaniel eyes. Those are gone.

The patients and I are meeting on an adult level. I am finding out what is happening to them, how they are coping with a life-threatening disease that comes in a hundred different forms, unpredictable and frightening. I'm being received as a person who has voluntarily stepped into their life orbit, just to be there for awhile if they like.

Ken with the riveting gray eyes commented that he appreciated my visits. He understood that this was an incidental part of my life. I told him frankly that I dream about the people in the hospital, think about them every day, that the visits are the most important thing happening in my life.

His steady eyes took me in as I said this. He understood. He used to volunteer with APLA before his own lover became ill and required all his energy.

Howard, the former dancer with the exceptionally beautiful hands, asked me what I thought was going to happen, would this devastating AIDS epidemic begin to be met with the necessary resources to find a cure and help for longer lives for those infected? How would the stigma against gays and lesbians be affected? I told him I didn't know, I only knew where I want to be on these issues: a voice for sanity, acceptance, and compassion. I'm doing what I can.

Every day or so changes are taking place inside me. Some are monumental, others small. I haven't had the energy to write about them.

The other day, Cecil and I were walking in the neighborhood. I shared an image with him, that subterranean rivers of my life were converging. As they flow together they are picking up power and threatening to collapse the surface. Cecil responded with surprising equanimity saying, "Maybe that's a good thing."

Because of the illnesses and deaths, some part of me does not want to go on, does not want to take the next steps. But actually being sick so much this fall has scared me. I don't really want to be sick and die. As hard as living is, it's what I want to do.

The morning after that conversation with Cecil I woke up and felt changed. At the breakfast table I told Cecil that some of the major compulsions in my life seem to be ending. I don't think I'm able yet to understand it. But my longing to have my father, dead now 16 years, and his many substitutes pay attention to me seems to have ended. Perhaps my frantic activity to create worth so that I might be loved was part of that compulsion. Engaging my life with the lives of these men who are facing their deaths has deeply affected me. Their allowing me to be a quiet presence in their lives when they have so little time left has been an affirmation.

I don't feel a weight of responsibility for seeming to have time yet to plant and to grow. I just see it as the way it is. My intention is to get well and get on with my life.

———◆◆◆———

Tuesday, September 26

I dreamt the Los Angeles Dodgers were playing in the stadium. Some or all the players had AIDS. The team was playing with the stigma of AIDS. There was some loss of support from the fans. But the team was playing very good baseball.

When I awakened from the dream and tried to remember it, I realized that I had not seen actual people playing ball. They had somehow been symbolized in my dream. And the dream had concluded indefinitely, the game was continuing to be played and was repetitive, as dreams are when we have a fever. I woke up because I wanted the dream to stop.

I think the dream was about my admiration for people living with AIDS, with some stigma, with the terrors and difficulties, doing their best. And I think it reflected my pain at seeing the epidemic continue on. I want the epidemic to stop.

Thursday morning, September 28

I'm still working out my feelings about engaging in the work of loving someone who is about to die, someone I have not known before and will know only for this brief time.

At the hospital Tuesday, I saw Roy again. He is terribly weak now, could only speak in a whisper, has had some memory loss. I had to lean close to him to hear what he said. When he was in the hospital just before I left on vacation in August, he was spirited, in fact, angry about some things that had happened in his treatment. I liked seeing his spirit. It was hard to see him this time so weak.

In the presence of actual people there is seldom a question of wanting to extend love and comfort. I guess the question can only arise after the person is gone and I'm missing them. Maybe I have some resentment that after I have invested love in them they up and die. It's irrational, of course.

I'm still feeling some of the pain of Mark's death. A book that's been important to me is "How Can I Help?" by Ram Dass and Paul Gorman. An important idea in the book is recognizing our own need to respond with love and compassion, and how that is rooted in a sense of basic unity with all people. That sense of unity reassures us that we are not frighteningly alone. I'm working hard on this, reading, praying, trying to understand my own needs. I want to continue this internal search so that I might become freer to care about others and less susceptible to burn-out.

I was re-reading some of this journal and noticed an entry for June 7: "… to be present as fully as possible in the moments life presents and then to let go and let the love and care we share do its own work." Maybe I need to look at this from the other way around. I think there is something I need to learn about letting go of someone and letting the love and care we have shared do its own work in my life.

Some people have a deficit in their metabolism so their bodies cannot take advantage of certain nutrients they take in. Perhaps I've been like that about the love and closeness that others feed to me. It may run right through me leaving only a trace behind. Perhaps that can be corrected.

━━◆◆◆━━

Wednesday, October 4

Today my friend Teresa Bremer asked me how the hospital visitation was going. I'm the kind of person who may not know what I'm thinking until I have to say it out loud. What I heard myself saying was that the visitation is going all right, but that it has been different since Mark died. I miss having a friend at the hospital.

━━◆◆◆━━

Thursday, October 5

I couldn't bring myself to go to the hospital this afternoon. So, I was home and rather accidentally watched a television program about families of AIDS patients. My friend Louise phoned and suggested I tune in. It was called "AIDS: Too Little, Too Late," about the importance of families being supportive and comforting to those who have AIDS. I cried through most of it. Then I wrote a letter to Mark's mother. I'd been meaning to do that. I cried through that, too.

I decided to go to the hospital after dinner to see Roy. God is a magician with a thousand hats from which to pull grace. Going to the hospital and visiting with Roy was one of the hats. We spent about an hour talking. The hospital is quiet in the evening, conducive to good conversation.

He held my hand.

80

We talked about death, which he was not afraid of, and illness, which he fears. And of changing perspectives about what a "long-term" goal might be. And the physical therapist in her early 20s who was gung-ho to get Roy well and strong again. And his friend who was diagnosed with AIDS and refused any treatment and was dead three weeks later and avoided all this suffering. And that Roy had been staying alive because it would break his mother's heart for her son to die.

And it wasn't a depressing conversation. It was rich and honest. Roy punctuated it with his good humor. But mostly it was serious. That doesn't mean sad, just serious.

I felt grateful for our time together and so did he. Thanks be to God.

Thursday, October 19

In my morning prayers I read a passage from the Brazilian theologian Ruben Alves' book Tomorrow's Child. "Let us plant dates even though those who plant them will never eat them. We must live by the love of what we will never see."

My first thought was for my own investment in loving strangers who would soon die. But then I realized that the people I have come to know as patients have planted dates they will never eat. Neal asking in the last hour of his life, "How are the other guys?" David setting aside his pain for a few moments to engulf himself in the fragrance of the freesias. Tommy in ICU, struggling for breath but trying to remember my name. Mark, in words and tears, sharing himself with me, a stranger who had stepped into his life quite incidentally. Hugh selling his motorcycle to buy a computer so he could write of his experience facing death from AIDS. Michael and Ken and Jimmy, all keeping courtesy and humanity alive to the end.

They planted dates they will not eat in this life. They are planted in the hearts and minds of lovers and friends and family and hospital staff, and in me. How shall I tend those dates planted in my mind and heart?

Sunday, February 18, 1990

It is winter. Last Sunday I was terribly depressed. I hadn't worked on this journal in weeks. I had taken a job to earn some money and the job wasn't working out for me, I was so exhausted in the afternoons when I got home that I couldn't write. I had given notice with no other job to go to and no prospects. I felt vocationally homeless, no place to go, no one expecting me.

At church, in that small company of saints, my community of faith for 20 years, everything affected me, a nerve pressed by the spine of life between indulgent misery and hope. In our friendship circle, a dear friend who is a gay clergyman made a special effort to move into the circle next to me and put an arm around my waist, as though to keep my spirit standing. We sang a closing hymn, "One Bread, One Body, one Lord of all, one cup of blessing which we bless. And we, though many throughout the earth, we are one body in this one Lord. Gentile or Jew, servant or free, woman or man, no more. Many the gifts, many the works, one in the Lord of all."

Tears flowed down my cheeks. I didn't sing, couldn't sing, could only look at the faces around the circle, faces of all colors, young and old, gay and straight, all of us just trying to make it, trying to find our place in the world. And I'm trying to find my place in the world. "Just be you," I could hear Mark saying. This is a congregation that welcomes some marvelous misfits, people of talent and commitment for whom society as it is does not work well. Rubbed wrong by life, the very rubbing can shape something of special value.

Being with that community prepared me to face another week on a job that wasn't a fit for me. I was ready to face another search for another job that would provide me income while I tried to finish a journal that nobody was waiting for.

That was last week. Now it's Sunday morning again. Sitting alone in the silence with intermittent sun slanting through the large window just behind me, sun that traded off with darkness and showers, it came to me that I've found in the men I have visited the value, the stories, the power in the face of great helplessness, that I long to know are in me, as well.

I have admired their determination to be valued, to act on their own behalf. Images crowded into my head of Mark and Hugh and others who were proud of who they were as gay men and never pretended to be anyone other than who they were. And fleeting recollections passed before me like images on "fast-forward" of some of the men when they were angry or insistent, making demands on nurses. Those patients were doing all they could to act on their own behalf. Mark, insisting that the damned beeping pole be removed from his room. Michael dismissing his doctor and getting another. Acting on their own behalf and being who they were.

These men are gone. But they left me a gift.

Through the morning and into the afternoon, I worked alone, sitting in my big reclining leather chair with my feet on the ottoman, writing notes on a yellow pad. I looked across the room into the dining room to a red rose in a bud vase on the dining table. Cecil gave me the rose for Valentine's Day. The rose was now dead. I wanted to go out and buy a fresh one for myself. The thought of buying myself a rose brought tears to my eyes. Through the years, I have acted on behalf of others, but seldom for myself. I have written many articles telling the stories of others, but not my own.

Why have I been visiting gay men with AIDS? I've been trying to discover my own value. Did I have value when I couldn't be the activist on behalf of other people? When Mark asked me direct questions which forced me to offer something of myself, my thoughts, my ideas and experience, he received me as one who has value just as I am. When they have offered me their stories, fears, hopes, they have valued me for just showing up — Pat Hoffman, 54 years old, with the body I have, the face I have, this human being, sitting with them in the gathering darkness which encompasses each of us, some slanting sunlight yet spilling over us for these moments. And in these moments we are still here, alive. I can hear Mark saying, "Just be you."

I think I always knew I had value but have been frightened to live out the life of my "true self." I have kept my true self, my true life in the closet like so many gay men. Out of shame or fear of rejection, I have hidden my thoughts and hopes. I have not led the cookie-cutter life society laid out for women of my generation. Yet I never felt free to be openly me. I would talk about myself, but with an evasive vagueness. I have been afraid to let myself know what I wanted from life, let alone go after it openly and with intentionality. Over the years, I've had my moments of strength and clarity, but they didn't last long.

I have identified with gay men and admire those who have led lives of risky integrity, out of the closet. And I've learned so much from those with AIDS, about taking as much control as I can over my own life, about "living in my own clothes," about struggling to offer whatever I have to offer under whatever circumstances.

This is my story, and my story links me to the stories of all these others, gay men with the dreaded disease of AIDS, men who even in their closing days have stories to tell, have beauty, and carry in their ravaged bodies a power to act on their own behalf and to affect those around them.

After a little while I went out to a florist shop near my house and bought myself a white rose with just a tint of blush near the center of the opening bud. I bought myself a rose and asked, "Will you be mine?" You 54-year-old woman with the tiny, hair-fine wrinkles set in around your mouth, with bad knees and no uterus and a little paunch where you used to have a flat belly. You, woman, with your secret hopes and dreams, with your very private sense of vocation, with your own story to tell. Please be mine while you still can be warmed by the sunlight slanting through the window.

"Why are you doing this work?" the patients have asked. "Do you have a son who is gay? A son or daughter who has AIDS?" No. I've done this work because I have needed help. I needed to find my way home to my own true self.

Conclusion

Five years after that last entry in my journal I was a chaplain intern in a hospital in Oxnard, California, sitting in a circle with six men affected by AIDS, leading a meditative reading of scripture. Candles flickered on the table in the middle of the room. In the quiet we were waiting on how God might speak to us in this passage from Matthew 11: "Come to me, all you that are weary and are carrying heavy burdens, and I will give you rest. Take my yoke upon you and learn from me; for I am gentle and humble in heart, and you will find rest for your souls. For my yoke is easy and my burden is light."

All the men in the circle had grown up in faith communities. None was now affiliated with a church. As we shared our reflections on the scripture one man rejoiced upon hearing good news in the passage. He said that all the messages he had previously heard from the church were of heavy burdens. Another man, raised in a conservative church in the Midwest, found the passage invited him back into the scriptures. Poignant for me was the man who frankly stated that he had had difficulty hearing an invitation in the passage. He had, however, in his silent meditation stayed with the experience of feeling blocked and realized it was because he was not accustomed to being invited to hear God's word. He told us it was the first time in a religious setting that he ever felt part of the circle, felt invited.

I was offering this spiritual meditation group during the last quarter of a year of Clinical Pastoral Education, a professional training program for chaplaincy. I entered the program to develop skills as a chaplain so I might bring some of the church's ministry to persons living with HIV infection and to the persons who love them. I also have a longing to help awaken more of the church to the need for ministry and service in the growing pandemic.

No one in the United States is untouched by AIDS, yet many feel uninvolved and believe that AIDS is not in their lives. But it is.

Last week I spoke with a couple whose son died at Daniel Freeman Marina Hospital in 1989. During their shock and grief over their son's death they chose to tell their congregation that he died of cancer. He did, indeed, have Kaposis' sarcoma. The husband said, "We chose not to offer the full story ... Now I wonder if [we] made the wrong decision. Would it have been better to sincerely help the congregation face the fact that one of its families had suffered through the tragedy of AIDS? But our own need was so great. We were not prepared to try and educate a congregation."

A few days later I was calling on the mother of a man who died almost a year ago in Ventura County, where I have been a chaplain to persons with HIV. This woman and her husband are active Baptists, as had their son been. In their case their congregation knew the son, James (not his real name), had AIDS. Some friends in the congregation had rallied to the support of the family and of James. But the senior minister condemned James from the pulpit and suggested that AIDS was God's punishment. It was a painful story that James and his mother had told me some months before James' death.

I went to call on James' mother because she was willing to share with me a letter James wrote, and apparently never sent, to his pastor. It was a civil and reasoned letter that, nonetheless, expressed his hurt and anger.

This family had let the congregation know that James had AIDS and then found some people needed educating. James' mother is still working on that project so that other families might feel more supported than she and her husband and son did.

Last Spring Patrick (not his real name) was close to death at the Ventura County Medical Center. Patrick asked his wife to phone me and ask me to come to the hospital. When I got there I found him very sick and agitated. He asked me to pray with him, which I did. He had once been a Roman Catholic and I offered to call a priest for him, but he declined. I asked if he was afraid and he said he was. I asked what he feared. He feared that he was not ready to meet God. When asked what was on his mind that he might wish to confess, he began a slow litany of three confessions. After each I offered him God's forgiveness and each time he thanked me. Then I gave him a blessing. The next day he slipped into a coma and died early Sunday morning.

Whether it is relatively well people in the spiritual support group or Patrick in the hospital, we are talking about people who are facing their mortality and are reaching out for spiritual support. Grieving families and friends are needing, longing for support and comfort in their losses.

But, like Patrick, they are not likely to turn to people and institutions from which they expect condemnation. And much of that condemnation, which even heterosexuals like Patrick feel, stems from the church's attitude toward homosexuality. And the stigma affects the grieving families, parents, brothers, sisters, aunts and uncles and cousins, and grandparents. How many are missing the comfort and support the church could give?

What do we know about where the HIV virus is spreading? Year by year the Centers for Disease Control and the World Health Organization report alarming increases in numbers of people diagnosed with AIDS. In the United States in January 1995 there were 401,789 AIDS cases reported. But these statistics reflect only the number of people with depleted immune systems. People infected with the virus, but well, are the larger part of the iceberg.

And if people — in and out of churches — have felt safe and removed from the problem of AIDS they need to awaken to the realities.

AIDS has become the leading cause of death in the United States among those aged 25–44. The largest increases in reported cases of AIDS, according to the CDC, have occurred among teen-agers and young adults, primarily through heterosexual transmission. In 1994 the American Medical News reported that females were showing the fastest-growing incidence of AIDS in the nation.

How is this information affecting you right now as a reader? Is your mind glazing over? Is it too much to register? Are you not wanting to think that you or your loved ones might be at risk?

As you reflect on this journal I hope it will help you to put faces on the statistics. Each person who is infected, each person who dies, is someone's son or daughter, someone's sister or brother, someone's husband or wife, mother or father, friend and loved one. We hide from this reality as a way to avoid feeling the pain.

But what is the price of that avoidance? For myself, I would never have wanted to miss meeting the people I have met, Mark and Bob and Alice, Tommy and Robert, Roy and his mother, and all the others at Daniel Freeman Marina Hospital and the people I have come to know here in Ventura County. As our lives have connected around issues of mortality, meaning and faith I have made discoveries about myself and my life has been deeply enriched.

Thomas Merton, a Trappist monk, writer and teacher, wrote in "New Seeds of Contemplation:"

"I must look for my identity … not only in God but in other people. I will never be able to find myself if I isolate myself from the rest of humankind as if I were a different kind of being."

As that is true for individuals it is also true for the church. The AIDS crisis with its reminders of our sexuality and passion invites us as individuals and as the church to break through our tidy illusions of who we are. It invites us to see ourselves more fully: in gay men and those who love them; in young women who may have used drugs or slept with men who did; in grandparents struggling to care for children orphaned by the epidemic; in people who had blood transfusions and are now living with the AIDS virus; in families living under the oppressive cloud of having someone they love suffering with AIDS.

Our identity as individuals and as the church affects what we are able to offer to others. Jesus' whole ministry spoke to this reality. He could empathize with the despised tax collector, with the prostitute about to be stoned to death, with the woman he met at the well, who had had several husbands, with the Roman centurion whose servant was ill. Jesus invited the "righteous" to drop their illusions about who they were and how good they were and to learn from him by following him into more associations.

In the midst of the AIDS epidemic God is again issuing an invitation. Not everyone will feel called to direct service with persons living with HIV. But an invitation is being offered to the church to faithfully bring the riches of its spiritual inheritance to people in need in the AIDS-affected community.

In the 16th chapter of the Gospel according to Luke we find Jesus' story of the rich man who ignored the poor man, Lazarus, who was suffering and hungry just outside the rich man's gate. The poor man died and was carried away by the angels to be with Abraham. Later, the rich man also died and found himself suffering in Hades. The rich man called out to Abraham asking if Lazarus could dip his finger in water and cool the rich man's tongue. But Abraham said the chasm was too wide and that Lazarus could not cross over. It was too late for the rich man to awaken to the importance of mercy. And, sadly, the rich man's family was also unaware of opportunities for turning toward grace.

My prayer is that the church with its wealth of spiritual resources for comfort and healing will offer these good gifts to people hungering and suffering in the AIDS-affected community, so that it may not be said of the church that it did not enter into God's blessedness because it failed to show compassion.

Prayers

Parents Prayer

Sorrow engulfs me.

This one whom I love,
from my very body,
is suffering and I cannot take the suffering away.

The sorrow is like a nightmare that will not end.

I pray that the end will not come — the death that will
rob my eyes of the sight of this one whom I love.

Yet every day I wonder if I can be sustained for
another day.

Comfort me.

You who cannot save me from the nightmare,

Be beside me.

PAT HOFFMAN

———•◦▪◦•———

Prayer for Transformation

How to live with the sorrow.
"I will pour out my spirit on all flesh"

Come Holy Spirit with the healing balm.
And may I receive it.
This balm of kindness and attention to my suffering.
A friend's touch.
Reception of my tears.
A good joke reminding me that belly laughs heal.

May I stay in the moment enough to absorb the warmth of
sunshine, the natural beauties meeting my senses.

May I be present to the comfort of routine,
the fragrance of breakfast,
the smell of hot soup,
the taste of bread.

May I recognize Your Spirit reaching out to support mine in
music which moves into my soul and lets it know itself and be
transformed.

Let me light these candles
and know that it is my hand lighting them.
I am alive.
Lead me to know my purpose now.

Move me from weeping to clarity of intent.
With this prayer I turn my face toward You.

PAT HOFFMAN

Prayers for Healing the Inner Self

Breath prayers are an ancient tradition, sometimes described as a prayer that is always present in your heart, like your very breathing. Breath prayers can be repeated, breathing in gently with the first portion and out with the second. (Breath in) ... (breath out)

In the quiet of my heart I find God present and able to help.
God present ... to help.

I am able to increase in wholeness in my inner person.
I am ... able.

In the love of family I see God's presence.
God present ... in love.

In the care of friends I see God's love.
God present ... in friends.

I desire to forgive people who have hurt me.
I forgive ... (name of person).

I earnestly ask for forgiveness for people I have hurt.
Forgive me ... for hurts (or name of person).

During this illness, lift my burden of fear. Increase my trust that
You are present with me and will sustain me.
Increase trust ... lift fear.

May I grow in confidence that I am in Your care,
in sickness and in health, in life and in death.
I am ... in Your care.

PAT HOFFMAN

Daily Prayers

The following prayers may be used with one for each day of the week. You might use one prayer at the beginning of each day and keep that day's breath prayer in your mind and heart throughout the day.

Day 1

The past feels so heavy: all that has hurt me; all those I have hurt. But Jesus came that we might have a new life. I pray, Lord, that You will help me to know that each day is a chance to begin anew.

Begin again ... in God's love.

Day 2

Dear Brother Jesus, I want to be Your disciple. Help me to accept what is past and begin again today, in Your love.

Walk with ... Jesus.

Day 3

I am remembering, Lord, people who have hurt me. I cannot change what they have done to me, but I pray that You will help me to forgive them.

Help me ... forgive.

Day 4

Dear Lord, at the beginning of another day I wonder what my life is about. Help me to find meaning in this day.

Help me ... find meaning.

Day 5

Dear Lord, I am often afraid. If I am afraid today, may I know Your holy presence with me comforting me.

Lord be with me ... comfort me.

Day 6

Lord, I have prayed that You will be with me. Help me search and know how I can be with You. May my reading of the Bible and interactions with other people bring me answers about how to be with You as part of Your community.

May I be ... with You, Lord.

Day 7

Dear Lord, I have had a lot of trouble in my life. It feels heavy to me, like carrying around a heavy load. The load would feel lighter, Lord, if I could take some of the troubles out of this sack on my back and use them for some good purpose. Help me find a way to make my troubled past serve some good purpose.

Use my past ... for good.

PAT HOFFMAN

Comfort from Fear

"For you did not receive a spirit of slavery to fall back into
fear, but you have received a spirit of adoption."

Romans 8:15 NRSV

Fear.
It separates me from You, God.
I guard my fears,
telling myself and others how they are justified.
While guarding my fears,
I allow time to slip in and rob me
of Your tender gifts:
A day of health.
The face of my friend.
The comfort of touch.
Give me one thing more:
Infuse me with Your Spirit
that I may attend to Your many gifts.
Forgive my fear.
Restore me to gratitude.

PAT HOFFMAN

Prayers of Trust and Acceptance

The following personal prayers may be used as morning and evening prayers. The breath prayer can be used during the day, keeping the prayer thought close like your very breathing.

Morning Prayer

I give thanks for this new morning. It is a gift from You. May I know my reliance on You, how fragile life can be. May I know today when I am anxious and accept those feelings. Take my anxiety into Your heart, compassionate God, and use it for Your loving purposes. May I know when I am worried and accept those feelings. Take my worries into Your hands and help me carry them. May I know when I need support and guide me to seek it. May I know my limits and know You will be there at the limits to take the load off my shoulders. Thanks be to You, O God.

Be with me ... comfort me.

Evening Prayer

The day of work is ended. The night is come. Hold me safe through this night. By Your grace may I be confident of Your presence in me and around me, in this place, and with those dear to me. Bring me the gift of slumber that I might be prepared to serve You another day.

PAT HOFFMAN

Testing Positive

POSITIVE

POSITIVE   Read the results

POSITIVE   Its presence confirmed

POSITIVE   What an absurd label

POSITIVE   For a death knell

POSITIVE   . . .

POSITIVE   I could adapt

POSITIVE   . . .

POSITIVE   Then the revelation

POSITIVE   Broke its barrier

POSITIVE   I was merely molting

POSITIVE   My earthly skin

POSITIVE   Freeing my eternal spirit

MATTHEW GARRISON

Prayer of Confession

God You promised to be my source
of courage, strength and wisdom
for these times.
FORGIVE MY UNBELIEF

You promised You would
never leave me or
forsake me.
FORGIVE MY UNBELIEF

You promised Your Grace
is sufficient in all things.
FORGIVE MY UNBELIEF

You promised You would
never leave me
comfortless.
FORGIVE MY UNBELIEF

You promised You would
instruct and guide me
in the ways I should go.
FORGIVE MY UNBELIEF

You promised I could trust You
to be my security.
FORGIVE MY UNBELIEF

Your promises never fail.
FORGIVE MY UNBELIEF

Help me claim Your
promises with the faith
and trust of a child.
Remind me to rest in You.

CAROL HAMILTON

A Prayer in the Face of AIDS

I've been running, God, but of course you know that.
I've been running away from HIV and those infected,
   from those living with AIDS and those dying from AIDS.
Of course my running hasn't been that obvious (or has it?)
   except to those few who see past my facade.

I have done all of the "socially acceptable" things,
   all of the "politically correct" things that one should do.
I have attended conferences and read articles,
I have gone to benefits and donated to garage sales.
I even volunteered and worked for AIDS organizations.

But, God, it's so hard for me to be with those who are sick,
   or who will probably become sick, with this insidious virus.
Perhaps I am afraid when I look into their gaunt faces
   that I am looking into my own face,
     seeing my body wasted away from disease or covered with lesions.

Perhaps I am running away from these sisters and brothers
   because I feel guilty that I have somehow (to this point)
     escaped the virus which has taken so many persons from me,
   or because to many I represent the institution which has
     shut them out, cut them off, cast them angrily aside.

I've been running, God, but of course you know that.
But I'm more tired of running now than I am scared of AIDS.

Help me, God, to find the courage and the strength I need
    to simply be myself with those infected and those sick,
        those fighting to live and those longing to die.

Help me, God, to see not only the bodies of those with AIDS,
    but to look into their hearts and souls as well.
Remind me again, God, how much I may receive from them,
    and how much these precious children of yours have to teach me,
        about myself and about you, about dying and about living.

PERRY W. WIGGINS

———◆+✳+◆———

A Stillness in Los Angeles

Sunset.
To begin: the seating of the body —
flesh that is my blood, bone, fate —
on the couch across
from the window. And the sky
full of red, full of the power
of coming night.

This sunset:
drama with no plot
I could ever write … in fading light
the fern on the coffee table
lifts its arching branches —
lifts a leafy fountain
flowing through the air

Growing darker:
Each narrow breath moves out — solitary road
I have been following, all along …
against the falling night, an airliner
flashes its brilliant lights — they are green, red,
white — high over the Pacific, high over
the moving waters.

Ivy Dempsey

Sitting

At ten o'clock in the morning
in a room without voices
I am sitting.
My hands do not move.

My eyes blink automatically
as I watch the elm trees
visible through the window —
their branches are thickly covered now
with young leaves, green and bright
as the word "summer,"
and these beautiful tall plants
swing and dip in a light wind
whose shape I am trying
to imagine.

I will know other rooms;
June is not the only month.
Will I learn, for my seasons,
how to leave it behind
in my year?

Sitting, let me ride my question
as a light wind.

Ivy Dempsey

Notes